Shelley Davidow is originally from South Africa but has spent the last two decades living and teaching in Europe, the Middle East and the USA. The author of forty books, she writes across genres. Her work includes children's fiction, award-winning young adult fiction, and adult non-fiction. Now based in Australia, she lives on Queensland's Sunshine Coast with her husband and son. Visit her website at www.shelleydavidow.com.

Bookclub notes for *Whisperings in the Blood* are available at www.uqp.com.au.

# SHELLEY DAVIDOW

# *Whisperings in the Blood*

UQP

First published 2016 by University of Queensland Press
PO Box 6042, St Lucia, Queensland 4067 Australia

www.uqp.com.au
uqp@uqp.uq.edu.au



Cover design by Sandy Cull, gogoGingko
Typeset in 12/16 pt Adobe Garamond Pro by Post Pre-press Group, Brisbane
Printed in Australia by McPherson's Printing Group

The publishers wish to thank Dr Jennifer Dowling for her assistance with the Yiddish passages in the book.

National Library of Australia
Cataloguing-in-Publication data is available at http://catalogue.nla.gov.au

ISBN
978 0 7022 5398 0 (pbk)
978 0 7022 5705 6 (ePDF)
978 0 7022 5706 3 (ePub)
978 0 7022 5707 0 (Kindle)

University of Queensland Press uses papers that are natural, renewable and recyclable products made from wood grown in sustainable forests. The logging and manufacturing processes conform to the environmental regulations of the country of origin.

# Contents

# PART ONE

The spring of 1913, and a young man from a remote village in Lithuania steals a ride on a train headed for the city. Everything around him has turned the colour of ash, as the cold seeps across the land, pressing any signs of life deep into the ground.

Perhaps it is written in his blood: a special code which will emerge later in someone else, generations into the future, in nightmares and fears; in someone's inability to breathe. In Vilnius, the frowning buildings as he arrives stop him from breathing.

He has a sense of impending tragedy. Maybe his lack of breath has to do with the act of leaving. And yet who would ache to leave this behind – this wasteland of grief and broken souls? Pogroms and nights of bloodshed and terror will live in him no matter how far he travels. Loss has encoded itself in the flow of his blood, in the beating of his heart – a ghost that will travel through time, through his DNA.

The future is already written, but he cannot read it. He can only sense its weight, its texture, and he has to believe that anything is better than this. As his life flashes by outside a fast-moving train, his past dissolves. The village and the 1800s have disappeared forever. The hours in the wig factory are gone. He hopes he will no longer feel he must apologise for the act of living. He hopes to shake the sense of being not a second- or third-class citizen but a tenth-class citizen – the lowest of the low. His shoulders will straighten. He will learn a new language.

His jacket is threadbare and the cold creeps in, tightening around him. He holds a leather bag in which he keeps parts of his soul: the memories of people left behind. Across his back he carries a gift from someone lost: the violin given to him by his father. All that is musical within him is held together in the case, wrapped with string so that it doesn't fall apart.

✡

Nothing can prepare him for the sodden ground of England, sprinkled already with flowers that look like fallen stars. His black jacket with its torn elbows suddenly turns blue in the light of early spring. He wonders how the grass can be so green. The language around him sounds like the twittering of birds. It is like the light: unimposing, forgiving – the music of a shallow stream rather than the rushing of a swollen river.

His destiny, after his arrival in England, is an accident of fate. He takes a step in one direction rather than in another. Boats are leaving for Africa, for Australia, for America. He takes the first available place he can find. Later, all the intricate unfoldings of generations, of lives and loves on several continents, can be traced back to a single moment: the one where he sets foot on the creaking hull of the SS *Graf Waldersee*, a steamship bound for America.

Three sisters have already taken boats to America.

The future reaches across and nudges him towards his new life.

✡

The young Jewish man who boards the ship holds his violin and his dreams on his lap when he sleeps. His name is Jacob.

New York is a giant even then: a well-dressed concrete-on-granite promise of a new life. Jacob's language sits in his throat like gravel. He looks at the signs and writing of a culture that seems simple, sharp and out of reach. The ghosts of the pogroms have half-drowned already in the freezing Atlantic.

*–Your name?*

*–Jacob.*

*–Place of birth?*

*–Sorry?*

*–Place of birth?*

*–No.*

*–Russia?*

*–No. Yes.*

✡

Almost seventy years after the young man boards the train in Lithuania, a girl sits on the steps of a thatched African farmhouse. On this day, the eleventh of April in South Africa, she's turning eleven. The morning sun has turned the veld green-gold. She woke at four, the time of her birth, and went to stare out at the sky. Billions of stars overhead rained down their light. A late moon dipped and set. She contemplated time and space until she was dizzy with infinity.

Granny Bee arrives, as promised, as early as she can. She hugs the girl and then sits next to her on the steps. She hands her a violin case.

*–Happy birthday, darling Shelley!*

*–Is this Dad's?*

*–Yeah, this is it. It hasn't been played for decades, but it's precious. You see, when your dad expressed an interest in playing the violin as a little boy, I told my own dad in Chicago … and though he had very little money, he bought this violin and sent it over.*

*–Did your dad play violin?*

*–Real well. I don't remember too much, though. He should have been a musician.*

*–But he was!*

*–Not a professional one. He gave some lessons and I believe he was a good teacher.*

*–I wish he could have been my teacher. What songs did he play?*

*–I have to think. Well, of course he played* Hava Nagila. *I remember that.*

*–Okay, I'll learn that one. Granny Bee, can you show me your tiny fingers?*

The girl's grandmother, whose bright skin is still smooth even though her hair has gone salt and peppery, lets the girl touch the pointer and middle fingers on her left hand. The umbilical cord wrapped itself around them before she was born and prevented them from developing. The fingers look to the girl like baked beans, or baby mice. She loves them.

*–Granny Bee, can we draw faces on them?*

Granny Bee doesn't share the enthusiasm required to turn the fingernails into faces.

*–When are you going to comb your hair, my girl? It's real messy.*

*Real messy.* Granny Bee's American accent is full and moist, the promise of some exotic faraway world. In the girl's heart, the sound of an imaginary violin expands until the beauty is overwhelming. It stops, and hangs in the air. Granny Bee says, *In America it's still the tenth of April right now. My mother died on the tenth of April, in 1927.*

The girl tries to imagine. The shape of a lost mother hovers for a moment inside her heart.

*–Is that why you went to the orphanage?*

*–Yeah. My dad couldn't care for us.*

*–Why not?*

Granny Bee doesn't explain. *At any rate, your birthday has made this day a happy one for me, darling.*

✡

Some months later, the girl sits on the steps again, waiting. Mr Miller, the violin teacher, is late. She hopes he's forgotten about her lesson. She opens the violin case and pulls out the instrument chosen by her great-grandfather, the violinist. Long ago, thousands of kilometres away, his hands held this. She imagines him playing a scale on the three-quarter-size instrument in some shop, thinking about his grandson in Africa, thinking, *Yes, this one sounds good.*

Mr Miller's white sedan arrives. It's brown with dust from the dirt road. In the way he confidently straightens his collar, it can be seen that he is an excellent teacher who will make certain that she corrects her lazy hold on the violin, her too-tight grip on the bow, and her slow progress reading music. She stands up. Her heart empties. The notes she will play today will be harsh and scratchy and often out of tune. They will elicit criticism and shame. They will not do justice to such a fine instrument. They will not fill her with their beauty and illuminate the world.

She doesn't know, as she stands there watching the teacher get his violin out of the back of his car, that this day will mark the end of months of lessons; that he will tell her he is wasting his time with her; that she will put the violin carefully back in its case, and leave it untouched for the next thirty years.

When she finally plays *Hava Nagila*, she will be thousands of miles away from those verandah steps and the house in Africa, and Granny Bee will long since have passed away.

Exactly a century after Jacob's arrival in America, his great-granddaughter, the girl with buried dreams of a violin, uncovers his story and the story of his daughter, the orphan girl. In bundles of letters tied with yellowed string, whisperings in the blood, passed down through the ages, voices from her ancestors, hidden from the light for so long, begin to speak.

As she unravels his story, it emerges as a series of opaque clues. Images drift into the gaps that history did not record, and flood them with life and colour. In the twenty-first century she rubs away the whitewash of time and uncovers pieces of her own soul embedded in some unrecognisable place. They tumble out unexpectedly – like resolutions that collide with each other at the end of a cheap paperback.

✡

At first, when Jacob arrives in New York and muddles his way through the paperwork that will make him a new citizen in a new world (by the grace of God), he believes he will learn to breathe again. But he knows that this breathing will not be a lifetime of deep inhalations; it will be the tentative takings of his new country's air. The sky is a wide, high blue, and the heat from the ground envelops him.

He has to make his way to Chicago, Illinois, where he finds his three sisters in rented quarters. When he knocks at the door and Rochelea opens it, colour drains from her face. She calls Saidie and Helen and then she falls over in a faint. Later she tells him they imagined he was dead. All this time and no word, not even a letter.

They have been living here for a year already. Jacob's dream was always to follow.

They usher him into the small living area, which seems luxurious to him, and strange. They tell him that they spend every Shabbos in a borrowed shul that is really a church. When they notice their father's violin case held together by string, the sisters are silent. Saidie wipes away tears. Rochelea explains to Jacob how hard it is to wrap her tongue around the unfamiliar shapes of the English language. *It doesn't fit*, she says. *English tastes too sweet, and has no depth. No one can understand my heart when I try to put it into these round words made of air.* Her struggle comforts him.

Jacob feels an embryonic joy that will never have the chance to illuminate his life. Grief is already written in the rough palms of his hands, in the fullness of his trembling lips, as he remembers jumping off the train in Vilnius, feeling the cold wrap icy tentacles around his heart.

Chicago does not embrace Jacob with any warmth. The buildings hunch away from him. The moment he opens his mouth to say anything, his lack of English defines him. The people are like the buildings, and recede from his incompetence in their mother tongue. He plummets into a void and cannot pull himself out. He is like many immigrants: needy, hardworking, talented, invisible.

So, it is hardly surprising that making a living is a struggle. The violin sits in its case. He travels across the country selling goods. In the warmer weather, he makes the most of the absence of ice and snow and expands his horizons. One day he is travelling with his horse and cart through Indiana. The wide prairies are behind him. A summer thunderstorm darkens the afternoon, and by the time he arrives at old Eli's farm, heavy drops of rain make small craters in the dust outside the house, and he knows by the sulphurous smell of lightning that he will stay the night.

✡

The soup is warm and, outside, the elements rage. Fields turn into a shimmering wave. But the wildness outside is nothing compared with the storm in Jacob's heart. Old Eli's daughter Ethel, the eldest of their nine children, reaches across the table to take his bowl from him.

–*Would you like some more?*

–*Sorry?*

–*No, no, I keep forgetting your English isn't that good.* Her laugh is bright, like her eyes. When she speaks English, he likes its softness. When she slips into Yiddish he notices that it's not yet a stranger's language to her.

–מער? *More?*

–קיין, דאנק. *No, thanks.*

Her smile is like the sun at the end of spring.

The last time he visited old Eli, he didn't take much note of his children still living at home. It seems that overnight one of them has turned into a woman. She is already twenty-five, but he doesn't know this then. He doesn't know that when the family boarded the ship to go to America, her brother Woolf, arriving late, took a ship to Africa, and that Ethel carries him tightly in her heart.

Jacob feels her hand brush his as she takes his bowl away, and the tempest in his heart threatens to blow him down.

He wishes that the storm might never end.

She moves through the room and demands no space. When he offers to help with the washing-up she is so astonished that her cheeks flush, and he feels the earth's slow turning.

After dinner, one of the children is playing the violin uncertainly. Staccato raindrops pummel the roof. Something stirs in Jacob. Before he knows it, he is standing by the boy, encouraging him in broken

English to keep the bows long, the fingers relaxed, the movement fluid. And when the boy finishes and hands Jacob the violin, lightning flashes and the image of Ethel, a dark-haired goddess standing in the doorway, is burned into his heart forever.

That night, music fills the house. Children trickle into the room. Old Eli and his wife let go of the heaviness of the farm for a moment. A candle, forgotten songs and a language that seems distinctly out of place at first create spirals of human warmth that swirl bodies into movement. Jacob's fingers have found once more the patterns and intervals, the rising and falling tones that are the sound of his soul. Ethel stops dancing after a short while, coughing, holding her chest. But her eyes are on fire. She leans, red-faced, against the stone wall.

✡

The storm rages on through the night and Jacob cannot sleep. But this agony is something to relish, a heightened sense that makes him dare to contemplate the unthinkable.

In the damp morning, just before Jacob leaves the farm, he asks Eli for his daughter's hand in marriage.

The proposal is made formal later through a marriage broker. This is how things are done. Jacob's sisters are distressed.

*–How will you afford to keep a wife happy?*

*–She will need many things that you can't give her. Trust me, women have many needs, especially in America. You cannot take a wife and then offer her nothing.*

*–But listen, please! She's not that kind of a person.* זי איז נים אַזוי. *Wait until you meet her.*

✡

The eleven-year-old girl who could not make beautiful music come out of the violin is still there three decades later, as I take the instrument, heavy with history, out of its case. I resist the desire to crumble into a past self. The dream from the night before is so strong that it moves me beyond my fear of failure and less-than-perfect intonation. In the dream, I was a solo violin-player and the music that emerged was a sweeping African dawn of effortless notes. I find the courage to begin a scratchy G-major scale. The teacher is kind. He is encouraging after the first five minutes.

–*Great intonation*, he says. *You'll see – it'll all come back to you.*

He looks at my fingers, which cling to the neck of the violin.

–*Relax*, he says. *The violin's not a life raft.*

But I fear that maybe it is. I tell him I'm very slow at reading music.

–*I don't want you to read the music. Close your eyes, and play me another scale.*

In the darkness, behind the flickering blacks and reds of my eyelids, there is no bow-hold, or grip, or intonation. The notes expand and swell and my fingers find their position. When I stop and turn to him, his eyes are like still ponds moved by a sudden gust.

–*Play me something you remember.*

–*I've forgotten it all.*

–*The body has a way of remembering. Try it. Think of the last thing you played.*

At first it's just one bar, something buried in the brain and remembered by the fingers. But then the whole phrase returns, and my heart carries the tune all the way to its end.

I open my eyes and look to him for disapproval. No doubt the sounds are still as scratchy and unbeautiful as they were almost three decades ago.

*–Sorry, that was really horrible.* I have to get in there before he does.

He shakes his head. *How can you say that about something you've played with your whole body, your whole soul?*

That night, from a resonant realm beyond my reach, the music of a violin plays through my dreams.

✡

Jacob's life has, until this point, followed a tragic curve. On the night of the attack, his neighbourhood was burned to the ground. His house was the only one left standing. Men came inside, seething with a hatred he could not understand. He watched from a cupboard while these men, whose faces were masks of hell, rained blows on his father's head, and he heard the last words of that gentle man:

*–In the name of God, what have I done?*

Jacob learned that you did not have to commit any crime to be punished by death.

His mother and sisters walked back from the edge of the ghetto through the ash in the early morning to find Jacob lying over his father's cold, broken body.

So, when the marriage broker informs Jacob that Ethel has accepted his proposal, he does not know what to do with the sudden exodus of butterflies from beneath his rib cage.

He carries the news with him quietly and delivers it to his sisters. They are dumbfounded, fearful. Jacob's salary has been scarcely enough for them all, and now he is adding another mouth to feed. He sees their distress. When he speaks, his voice is like the breeze, light, disturbing nothing.

*–Now, now,* he says, as if they were still children. *I've taken care of you already. The marriage broker will find you suitable husbands, and*

*you won't have to worry any longer. He tells me there is a great demand for our kind of Jew.*

*–What kind of Jew is that?*

*–The Gefilte Fish Ashkenazis are coveted.* His smile is a rare ray of light in the room.

*–Why do they call us Gefilte Fish Jews? It's rude!* עס איז גראָב!

*–It's a compliment. Our tastes are less intense, less crass, less … oh, I don't know. Apparently we have a reputation for being intellectual. Apparently many new immigrant men want to better themselves, marry up. I have no idea why.*

*–I don't want to be married. And I'm not intellectual.* This is one point they agree on.

*–You can't be spinsters forever.*

Saidie puts down the sock she has been darning and walks out of the room. In the gust of her wake, the paraffin lamp flickers and goes out.

That is the longest conversation Jacob will have with his sisters for many years. He knows he will never win, and anyway, their understanding of the necessity of what must happen in life transcends their annoyance. He smiles again. His marriage is sealed. The delicate flower of hope for his new life awaits. As he is coming to believe – God will provide.

For the next three months, as he exchanges letters with Ethel, his heart swells with a new and unfamiliar sensation. It is as though, unaccustomed to joy, his heart feels pain every time it fills. He wonders whether seeing Ethel again will begin to heal something in him. In this no-man's-land between bachelor and married man, Jacob takes up his violin. Every night he drives his sisters crazy. They complain half-heartedly and he knows they don't mean it. In the music, and the rhythm, and the rich notes played on the D-string, which has a particular resonance, the voice of their father whispers its love, and no one has any real desire to silence it.

✡

In the hours when the night is heaviest just before dawn, I dream that I am about to play the violin. I take it out of its case and in my hands it comes apart. The bridge has collapsed and the strings hang loosely over the body of the instrument. The bow is in tatters and I have no idea how I am to make music on such a useless instrument. But I pick it up anyway and place it in the hollow curve between shoulder and chin, and the sound I make is as rough and raw as a torn soul. I feel tears burning in my throat. This is the furthest from beauty.

When I wake up in the morning, I stumble out of bed and go downstairs. I take out my gleaming wooden instrument and hold the bow as if it is a gift from another world. Moved by the fleeting brightness of an older dream and the words from my teacher, I close my eyes, dispel the shadows and slide the bow over the strings, thinking of the flow of water, the way the prow of a ship displaces the waves and moves single-mindedly towards its destination.

✡

The day that Ethel and Jacob get married is drenched in sunshine. Even Jacob's sisters are smiling. Ethel is an angel in white who floats beside Jacob, an apparition of joy so brief that in the span of history's long narrative, she is a single line on a page.

At first they all live together. But soon Jacob's savings allow the newlyweds to move out into their own house. Jacob peddles fruit and vegetables and odds and ends. English fluency eludes him. When he puts on his new language and tries to wear it, he is like a man attempting to dance in square wooden shoes. His soul resists its lightness. But love softens the cold and brightens the long, dark days.

His world is transformed by the arrival of a daughter who lies in her crib, a pink treasure from a faraway world.

Ethel is thirty years old. She is concerned because the baby has two tiny deformed fingers. They are little stubs. When she came out, her umbilical cord was wrapped tightly around the fingers.

–*She has strangled fingers*, Ethel tells Jacob. *Children will be cruel to her.* But Jacob hushes her and shakes his head.

–*She is perfect.* זי איז גאַנץ.

He is so besotted with his daughter that he hardly sees how pale Ethel looks, how she struggles. She has been diagnosed with diabetes. He kisses his daughter's forehead. *Bertha*. They whisper her name.

איך וויל צען קינדער.–

–*Ten children! I would never survive. Besides, we couldn't afford it.*

–*But at least one more!*

–*Jacob!* She laughs, and her reprimand has no conviction.

He can't help himself. His love for his family is an insatiable hunger. He wants more – more of this family, this warmth. Under his skin, the terror of losing something so dear hovers there like a ghost. Perhaps it's because of the losses of the past that he can't get enough of what he already has. He wants to hold Ethel, be near her, touch her. But often she pushes him away. She's tired, he thinks. It's because of baby Bertha, this miracle from heaven whose round face dents the pillow. And the price for this miracle is that his wife sometimes turns away from him.

One wintry day, Jacob receives the news of his father-in-law's untimely death. Old Eli stopped at a railway crossing with his horse and cart to light a cigarette. He didn't hear or see the approaching train.

Ethel mourns the loss of her father, who is soon buried in the Hammond Cemetery. But little Bertha demands love and life and laughter. In the months that follow old Eli's death, Bertha learns to stand, to walk, to talk; her mother's grief is overshadowed by fierce adoration when she holds the tiny hand with its strangled fingers and steadies her toddler on the sidewalk outside the house.

Three years after they have Bertha, Jacob's wish is granted. Ethel gives birth to a little boy. Jacob holds him close to his heart. *Meyer*, they call him.

Money is always scarce. The small house in Hammond, Indiana, has no running water and no heat. The horse and wagon wait patiently behind the house for Jacob each day. Ethel joins the socialists and pours her energy into fighting for the rights of the poor. *We are on our own*, she says. *No one will help us except ourselves. My father managed a flax factory in Kovna Gaberna but came here so that we could have a better life. We deserve respect and fair treatment, and we can't sit here and wait for those things to be given to us. We must take them.* Words, English words, bend to her will, and those around Ethel admire her. Some are even envious of her dedication and sharp intelligence. But her fire, her passion for social justice, consumes its source – like a candle.

Ethel hides her struggle with diabetes to avoid expensive medical attention. Then, her neck thickens. The doctor tells her she has a goitre – an enlargement of the thyroid gland. She has to step back from the causes she believes in so strongly. The icy reach of winter's breath creeps under the door of the house in Indiana.

Jacob and Ethel often argue. Below the surface it's about money and survival. Jacob is unable to be a harsh businessman, the reason for his arguments with Ethel. His customers shake their heads at his generosity, but they still accept it. He lets people owe him money, which they never repay. If he sees that someone needs vegetables and fruit he accepts their assurance that the payment will come next time. But all too often it doesn't.

The children begin school. They sometimes speak Yiddish at home, but Bertha and Meyer are immersed in a world of English words and the language rushes out of them – waves surging onto a familiar shore. Jacob is offered a position to sing at the local shul. His voice has a mesmerising resonance that echoes the vibrations of the violin. But the act of surviving has sapped his soul and he declines, though his heart yearns to do it.

The tragedy happens later.

When Ethel gets sick it seems trifling at first. Just a cold. But quickly, her thin body, weary with its battles, succumbs without much of a fight; the cold becomes a cough, bronchitis and then pneumonia. She is just forty. She whispers to Jacob one night: *Write to Woolf in South Africa. Tell him I'm very sick.* She will not make the trip to the hospital because it's too expensive.

When he wakes up on April 10, 1927, a Sunday morning, the children are still asleep. Beside him, in the bed, the one he has loved, the soft shape of his soul, is dead. Her name is a freezing whisper on his lips. *Ethel*, he says. His heart turns to ice.

He will never recover. At first, he will dissolve in grief. When he finally pulls himself half-together, his sisters will insist that he cannot afford to properly care for his two young children. They will have the next and last long conversation. Then, they will make arrangements: the children will be taken to the Jewish Orphan Home.

He will visit them sporadically, taking on menial jobs to keep alive. He will be a nightwatchman, which will be a better use of time than lying alone in the darkness with the ghost of his wife lost to death and the images of his children lost to life. He will escape by playing music to himself in the hollowness of the day. He will even teach the violin to other people's children. Jacob's enormous soul will try to confine itself to the perimeters of life's harsh demands.

When he dies, his entire savings, which he had imagined might ease his children's lives, will be claimed by the government of his adopted country.

He will leave nothing behind but his love, recorded in a single sentence uncovered in the twenty-first century by his great-granddaughter.

Lithuania: the train, the young man and the beginning of a new century.

And now this breaking of dreams.

STATE OF ILLINOIS )
) SS.
COUNTY OF COOK )

IN THE CIRCUIT COURT OF COOK COUNTY, ILLINOIS
COUNTY DEPARTMENT - PROBATE DIVISION

| | | | |
|---|---|---|---|
| ESTATE OF | ) | NO. | 68 P 9814 |
| JACOB FRANK | ) | DOCKET | 724 |
| DECEASED | ) | PAGE | 454 |

FINAL ACCOUNT

To the Honorable Robert Jerome Dunne, Judge of Said Court:

The undersigned, SYLVIA TARRE, Administrator With the Will Annexed of the ESTATE OF JACOB FRANK, DECEASED, respectfully submits to this Honorable Court the following as a true and correct accounting of all receipts and disbursements of the said estate, from the time of her appointment, to-wit: August 8th, 1969 unto the present:

RECEIPTS

| INVENTORY ITEM | SOURCE | AMOUNT |
|---|---|---|
| 1 | Savings Account No. 221754 in Harris Trust and Savings Bank | $ 8,469.12 |
| | Interest to August 19th, 1970 | 455.18 |
| 2 | Savings Account No. 118673 in Sears Bank and Trust Company | 3,485.79 |
| | Interest to August 19th, 1970 | 185.34 |
| | TOTAL RECEIPTS | $12,595.43 |

DISBURSEMENTS

| VOUCHER | PAYABLE TO - REASON | AMOUNT |
|---|---|---|
| 1 | Weinstein & Son Funeral Chapel - funeral expense | 207.00 |

| | | | |
|---|---|---|---|
| 4 | Harris Trust and Savings Bank - safety deposit box rental | | $ 33.00 |
| | COSTS OF ADMINISTRATION: Clerk of the Circuit Court of Cook County: | | |
| 5. | Filing fee | 16.00 | |
| 6. | Costs to date (Inventory) | 30.00 | |
| 7. | Certified copies of Letters | 5.00 | |
| 8. | Final Costs | 30.00 | |
| | | | 81.00 |
| 9, 10. | United States Fidelity and Guaranty Company - bond premium | | 216.00 |
| 11. | Harry Kaplan - witness fee | | 15.00 |
| 12. | Sylvia Tarre - witness fee | | 15.00 |
| 13. | Official Reporting Service - (Will and Heirship) | | 21.00 |
| 14. | Law Bulletin Publishing Company - (claims) | | 27.00 |
| 15. | Sylvia Tarre - Administrator With the Will Annexed Fees | | 625.00 |
| 16. | Martin M. Ruken - Attorney's Fees | | 875.00 |
| 17. | Chicago Board of Health - (Certified Copies) | | 8.00 |
| 18. | ILLINOIS DEPARTMENT OF PUBLIC AID - payment of claim (6th class) | | 10,053.53 |
| | TOTAL DISBURSEMENTS | | $12,595.43 |

RECAPITULATION

| | |
|---|---|
| RECEIPTS | $12,595.43 |
| DISBURSEMENTS | $12,595.43 |
| AVAILABLE FOR DISTRIBUTION | $ -0- |

Respectfully submitted,

Sylvia Tarre

SYLVIA TARRE, Administrator With the Will Annexed

✡

Before ten-year-old Bertha Frank can find a way through the tidal wave of loss, a man from the Jewish Orphan Home in Cleveland, Ohio, comes to take her and Meyer away. At that moment, he is simply a Taker. When she leaves home that November, her father's eyes are a desperate black. Jacob is silent. Perhaps the silence is a lack of adequate English words for his American children.

Generations later, Bertha's granddaughter will hear some of his whispers, a soft murmur, in her own heart.

At the train station in Cleveland, a man with black hair, black-rimmed spectacles and flecks of kindness in his eyes meets the man who is the Taker. He holds the orphans' hands in his, standing between them, a warm, solid presence.

–*I'm Jack Girick*, he says. *You'll be okay.*

In the orphanage, in the girls' dormitory in a building housing hundreds of Jewish orphans, Jacob's ten-year-old daughter lies awake at night on a single metal creaky bed. Her mother is dead. Dead. Life will never be normal again. Water pipes chug and creak through the endless night hours. Shadows stand over her. Bertha struggles to imagine her mother's face. She thinks of her father: because he is alive, she is anchored to a past. She can't remember the Yiddish words he used to say to her, but violin music plays quietly in her soul. She traces a journey that leads to now, and holds on to thoughts of the violin-player so that she does not fall through the hole in her heart where her mother should be.

Bertha imagines her father leaving his country, escaping the pogroms. She wonders what it's like to run away from death in your own country and then find death in your new home in your new country.

At first she is as insignificant as a single grain of sand in a shifting desert. Surrounded by two hundred children who have lost their parents, Bertha should feel an immediate bond with the others. She watches with envy as Meyer, with his winning smile and warm heart, endears himself to everyone. Only he is too talkative. Right at the outset he is struck on the back of his head by one of the adults for talking too excitedly before dinnertime. She feels a burst of hatred and helplessness. Her father would never have struck either of them, ever. She buries her anger, and minutes later her brother is in good spirits again, although he shows her the bump that swells at the back of his head to the size of an egg.

Bertha huddles against the chill on a Friday afternoon and hates the cold. The Jewish Orphan Home has been her home for three weeks. On the horizon, the last orange streak of the winter sun still remains. In Ohio the snow lies inches deep and the wind cuts through any number of clothing layers. The imposing building, with its dusty red brick and white columns framing the heavy front doors, looks like a haunted castle. It even has a tower. The building has five storeys. Behind it, the boys' and girls' wings are separated by a large courtyard. Bertha counts the windows that cover the front of the building. The façade is severe, but solid. It has no beauty but it protects them all from the worst of the outside world – not unlike the adults who take care of them. She circles around the fountain at the entrance, leaving tracks in the snow, and then creeps back along the wall towards the girls' wing.

*–What are you doing here? It's dinnertime.*

A girl with close-cropped hair, which makes her look like a boy, grins at her.

*–I might ask the same thing. Who are you anyway?*

*–I'm Gert. Gertrude Fogelson. Pleased to meet you.* She sticks out

her hand. Her fingernails are dirty. Bertha declines the hand and Gertrude drops it.

–*Bertha Frank.*

–*Nice. Gert and Bert. Don't you like that? Are you Meyer's sister?*

–*You have a lot of questions.*

–*Well, are you?*

–*Yes, I am. How do you know him?*

–*Everyone knows him. He's a friendly boy. So you two are new here. Your parents dead?*

–*My mom.*

–*I'm sorry.*

Bertha looks away from Gert's inquisitive face and continues creeping along the wall of the building.

–*What about your dad?*

–*He's too poor to take care of us.*

–*Yeah, well my dad's dead and Mom can't take care of us either and you have to learn to do the best you can with what you have. C'n I call you Bert?*

–*Sure.*

–*Say, you hear about Captain Hawthorne Gray? He reached the world's highest altitude ever in a balloon. Over forty-two thousand feet … in Illinois too! Then he had to parachute out at eight thousand feet.*

–*You sure talk a lot.*

–*Yeah, I know. But it stops me being lonesome. So, what do you think of Captain Hawthorne Gray?*

–*I don't care to talk about him. It's sad. He died doing that.*

–*But I'm thinking, wouldn't it be swell to see the world from that high up! I'd love to go up in a balloon, and travel far, far away … see distant lands and all that. You?*

–*I'm getting cold.*

*–C'mon. I'll show you how to get in before anyone notices you're missing. Avoid punishment at all costs.*

Gert reaches out to grab Bertha's hand, and Bertha shrinks away. She fears Gert is shallow.

*–I don't have the plague, you know!*

Bertha tucks her hands into her armpits and hides her fingers. But Gert's quick eyes have already perceived something amiss.

*–Did you lose your fingers or something? I guess you're ashamed. But you shouldn't be. Show them to me, will you?*

Gert has worn her down. Bertha sighs and holds out her hands, revealing the tiny, half-size fingers on her left.

*–It's a birth defect*, she says. *I haven't lost any fingers. The umbilical cord strangled them when my mother was pregnant, so they didn't grow.*

*–I reckon it's not a defect. I reckon it sets you apart and makes you special. C'mon, we'd better hurry.*

Before Bertha can argue against Gert's treatise on what makes people special, Gert has her by her deformed hand.

The two orphans do not know that this moment marks the beginning of their friendship – a bond that will survive international and civil wars, a continental separation, illness, love, marriages, births and deaths over the next seventy-three years.

✡

I am the girl who gave up the violin at eleven, but its music remains somewhere beneath my skin. Because of ships to America and to Africa, accidents of destiny, I am born below the equator in a country with iron-oxide earth, beating night-drums and tawny-eyed lions.

I take my first steps behind a split-pole fence on a soft lawn. On the other side of the fence, the musical waterfall of African languages rushes down the street. Women call out in high-pitched voices and men throw volleys of words like pebbles back at them as they head towards the gated compound for black workers at the end of William Road.

Africa's rhythms pulse through my childhood: the thunder of an afternoon storm; the distant drums of a Zulu dance; the throbbing of persistent crickets in the black night. My soul reaches deep into the earth and clambers up into the acacia trees and baobabs. It creeps under the grass and wraps around the zebras and giraffes. It harnesses sounds and presses them into my brain before I have words for them. It grasps the joy in the song of the piet-my-vrou bird and the dry smell of elephant dung when we walk through the bushveld. My feet are broad and covered in dirt. I swear to the sky every day that I will never leave this place.

✡

Mr Michael Sharlitt is the superintendent at the Orphan Home. He has hooded brows and thick lips. He tells the children that, as a former orphan himself, he understands their emotional needs. But he is regarded with trepidation. Everyone knows that the ultimate punishment is not being caned, quarantined or divested of privileges, but being sent to Michael Sharlitt's office.

He tells the children that the orphanage is moving to University Heights, in Cleveland's east. There will be cottages for everyone to live in. Twenty-five children in each cottage will be cared for by a cottage mother. This is supposed to mimic, as closely as possible, a family environment. Gert whispers:

–*Maybe we won't be treated like prisoners or like inmates in an asylum anymore.*

–*Hush up!*

The Sharlitt eyeballs are upon them and Bertha barely breathes.

✡

So, after two short years in the imposing brick building, Bertha and Meyer, together with a sea of children of Eastern European descent, move to the new orphanage, Bellefaire.

Bertha and Gertrude find themselves in cottage number nineteen. The cottage mother is a dragon, but they don't mind at all. They have each other. Where Bert is careful to be polite, Gert is outspoken and tactless. Bert resists voicing her opinion and keeps her sparkling self under wraps; Gert resists shutting up. It is a match made in heaven. The cottage mothers are there six days a week, but on Sundays they're replaced with cottage fathers. Activities are different with the Sunday Surrogates. There are ball games and races and a relaxed atmosphere that makes the orphans ecstatic.

*–Just goes to show. It doesn't have to be miserable, does it? Why can't the cottage mothers be as fun?* Gert points out. Bert has similar sentiments but keeps them to herself.

Meyer tells his sister that the boys in number fifteen have learned how to position their windows to catch reflected glimpses of the girls undressing. Bertha ensures her privacy from prying eyes but doesn't breathe a word to anyone about spying boys. Her allegiance to Meyer goes beyond her distaste at his friends' activities.

Bertha feels the cold. Gert doesn't, so at night she places her wool blanket over Bert's feet and steals back to her bed. And because Gert hates jelly and ice-cream (they make her cough), Bert, who is always hungry, gets extra on Friday nights.

Orphans are scrubbed shiny clean every morning at six and then, after chores, are bussed to regular state schools, where they interact with other children. With the move, the orphans have changed schools, and the new environment offers new challenges. Maybe she wasn't aware of it before, but they are set apart, the 'home children'. The other children's insults tear into Bertha's scars, already as deep as canyons. Being motherless means to long for normality with such desperation that it becomes a deformity of the soul.

Bertha finds that the most effective defence against the insults is silence and a cultivated exterior of calm. At the end of the school year, she is walking to class with Gert when they see a schoolyard fight between a home girl and another girl from the same class, who has been catapulting insults at her. The other girl says:

*–You're nobody and you have no home and no family and you'll end up in the filthy streets! You're so low.*

Bertha has emerged from the immediate heaviness of the loss of her mother. Now a rage against injustice burns beneath her skin. Her face flushes.

*–What are you doing, Bert? Don't get involved! We're all gonna get it if you—*

*–Excuse me a moment,* Bertha says, and wrests her arm away from Gertrude's.

She sees the distress on the home girl's face and turns to her smirking opponent.

*–You back right off now, you hear? She has a family, and it's a bigger one than you'll ever have.*

She takes the home girl by the arm and guides her away.

*–You don't have to take that from them, you know. Anyway, I'm Bertha, and this is Gertrude, and we're in cottage number nineteen at the home.*

*–Hi. And I guess thank you. My name's Arleen. Usually I'm of the belief that sticks and stones can break my bones but words can never harm me. Well, today I was wrong.*

*–Stick with us,* Gertrude says. *Safety in numbers. Cheer up, Arleen. Words can only harm you if you let 'em. I'll tell you a funny*

*story: you hear about Milt? He got caught, but what a laugh! He was in the metal workshop and he made a master key which allowed him to get into the kitchen … and each night for ages he sneaked into the kitchen, made up ten fried-egg sandwiches and then scaled the fire escape and handed the food to his pals. He got the belt, of course, but I heard he still has the key!*

*–Gert talks a lot.*

*–I do. But it's all true, isn't it?*

The earth turns and the seasons ripple across the land. Springs turn into summers overnight. The frigid air gives way to a blanket of humidity and Ohio suffocates in its own steam. On Saturdays, Bert and Meyer pool their minimal financial resources, which they earn from small jobs, and go to the pictures. They can afford two tickets and popcorn. Gert catches wind of this and tags along.

Bert's stomach is never satisfied. It growls and aches with hunger and feels like it's eating itself, even though the underweight kids, much to the envy of every other orphan at the home, get extra jelly to fatten them up. Meyer saves everything he earns and surprises his sister with treats as often as possible. As the older sister, she wants to take care of him, but her soul depends on his buoyancy, on his ability to surf the tide without sinking. With that support, she blossoms. She attracts the nickname Smiley. She knows every film, every film star and every famous scene, and can be relied upon to provide extravagant amounts of useless information on the on-screen lives of a host of celebrities.

The hot summer evenings go on forever. Gert and Bert walk arm in arm under the trees.

*–Berty, imagine, fifty years from now, these trees will be huge. These sticks will turn into oaks and line the walkway with shade.*

*–And we'll be old.*

*–Not that old. We'll probably be long married – with kids, oh my. And we'll be able to bring them here and walk them down a long shady avenue.*

*–Yeah.*

*–What do you want to be, Berty?*

*–Oh, I don't know. Happy, I guess.*

*–Don't you want to be married, and have a swell home, a handsome husband, and great friends? I do.*

*–Honestly, I have no idea what will make me happy.*

*–You could be a star in the pictures, you're that pretty. Just a bit thin, if I might say.*

*–You might not!*

*–Well, I just did!*

*–I like these trees, Gert. They'll be like our ghosts. Long after we leave, they'll be here, whispering our secrets to future generations.*

*–Oh, promise me we'll always, always be friends. I just couldn't stand it if we weren't.*

*–Of course we will!*

*–I reckon we should live in the same neighbourhood so we can celebrate Shabbos and Channukah and Pesach and everything together. Like family. I hate the idea of being far away from you.*

✡

It is around this time, after the orphans have been in the new home for just over a year, that Jacob pays them a visit. He has moved to Cleveland and found a job as a nightwatchman to be near his children. He wears a white hat with a black band around the middle and – even in the heat – a jacket and tie, his respectable clothes. Before he sees the children, he removes his hat and threads the rim repeatedly through his fingers. Meyer sees him and runs over, throwing his arms around him.

*–Daddy!*

*–Hello, son.* His hug is tentative. His voice is cracked. *Where is your sister?*

Meyer laughs. *That's Bert! Don't you recognise her?*

Bertha is wearing a white and green dress and black knee-high stockings. She holds her chin higher than necessary, clasps her hands behind her back and leans against the red brick wall of the building for support. Her thick hair is curled away from her face. Her jaw and cheekbones seem angular in the afternoon light and he cannot recognise her. She is almost as tall as he is. He notices she has her mother's forehead.

*–Hello, Daddy.*

*–איך האָב עפּעס פֿאַר איר ביידע.*

The Yiddish sounds like an old forgotten song. He sees the blankness on his children's faces and repeats himself in English.

*–I bring you somethings. A present.*

He fumbles in a brown bag and pulls out a book: *The Hebrew Bible – the Old Testament.*

Their mother's name is inscribed inside.

*–Thank you very much.* Bertha feels polite as she takes the book. As though her father is a stranger. She realises for the first time that he speaks English with a thick accent.

Jack Girick is there that day with his camera.

*–Stand over here, will you? I'll take a picture of the family.*

The word 'family' is heaviness. Bertha stands next to her brother. She feels the distance between herself and her father, and there is no way to reach out across the void and close the gap.

When her father leaves, a cold wind blows shut the door to a compartment in her heart so that it does not fill up with memories and break. She watches him go. Then she and Meyer run off to show Gert and Arleen their present.

✡

Soon after this, Jacob moves to Chicago, where there is more opportunity for work. In the big city, he sees his sisters on Friday nights. He walks down Milwaukee Avenue and recites the English street names to himself as he crosses them, listening to the intonation, to the music in the names, thinking of his children's voices.

He does not know that the colour of his soul is embedded in their hearts – a seeping ink-dark blue that will leak down through generations.

✡

Because of boats, families disperse. Lives dissipate into threads that wind themselves around new languages and continents. When Jacob took the SS *Graf Waldersee* to America to follow his sisters, Ethel was already there, and their lives collided in this new land. Ethel's brother Woolf had visions of following the rest of the family to America. But the ship that had room for him wasn't going to

America, and beggars couldn't be choosers.

Woolf's boat, the SS *Ionic*, left England in 1913, and followed the curve of Africa to its southernmost tip. It deposited him under the black skies and the Southern Cross on the edge of the Dark Continent. In Lithuania, his father owned a flax factory, so he took the surname Braker, after a part of the machinery in the factory. The name fitted more easily into the English-speaking world than Yalowitz.

After running the Olifant's River Trading Store in South Africa for twelve years, Woolf receives a letter on brown paper, written in Yiddish. The ink is smudged.

This is how he discovers that his sister Ethel is dead.

✡

An hour after supper, and already it's been dark for what feels like an entire day. Winter nights in the orphanage are seventeen hours long. Bertha lies shivering under the covers and Gert sits on her feet.

–*You know Al?* Gert says. *I was just talking to him the other day at school and let me tell you, Bert, all he wanted to know about was you. I had so many interesting stories to tell him. Do you know he wasn't even interested when I told him that the Cleveland Clinic fire last year was caused by X-ray film too close to an exposed light bulb and that most of the victims suffocated from the gas? No, all he wanted to know was how old were you exactly and what your favourite colour was and whether he should ask you to come to his baseball game. I told him 123 people died, but you think he could care less?*

–*He's Meyer's friend.*

–*And?*

–*He's only twelve.*

*–And you're thirteen! Anyhow. He gave me two cookies that he and a friend pocketed after Shabbos, but I had to promise that we'd both go and talk to him at recess on Monday. I saved one for you.*

Gert reaches into her pinafore pocket and pulls out a barely recognisable version of a cookie. Her voice drops to a whisper and she checks the door. Everyone's getting ready for lights out, and the dragon will appear at any moment.

*–To cheer you up. Eat quietly.*

*–Gee, thanks, Gert. But it's bribery!*

*–Of course it is! Within reason, Bert, one does what one can to make life bearable. Now eat up, will you?*

Bert is an expert at invisible eating. Her hands pass in front of her mouth like a magician's. The sugary crunch is heaven, and for five full minutes, there is no thought of cold, or hunger, or the dragon …

… who comes flaming into the room, barking the obvious:

*–Time to pray. Lights out, girls.*

And so, at recess on Monday, Gert, Bert, Arleen and Al find themselves huddling inside the cafeteria next to the classroom, while snow blankets the world outside and hardier souls have snowball fights in the schoolyard.

Al blows on his hands and Bert hides hers under the table.

*–Meyer and me, we're gonna join the army when we get out of high school,* Al announces. His face is thin and narrow. Bert thinks he's sweet.

Arleen ignores him.

*–Bert, what were you doing in Sharlitt's office on Thursday?*

*–Getting a letter from my dad.*

*–What did Sharlitt have to say?*

*–Not too much. He was gracious.*

*–That's Bert for you, Al. The Berty of few words.*

She doesn't say that Jacob's letter tells his beloved children their Uncle Woolf in South Africa (married to Dora Davidow) sends greetings to his nephew and niece. Included is his address. Bertha hides the letter in her precious box. She likes the alliteration in the sound of her aunt's name and whispers it to herself.

While Al chatters on about joining the army and seeing the wide, wide world, Bertha imagines how in the word 'Africa' there is so much heat and bright sun, enough to melt all the snows of every winter she has lived. She closes her eyes and sees flashes of zebra stripes in a shimmering savannah.

She contemplates writing a letter to her Uncle Woolf and Aunty Dora. Only she cannot picture what would be in it.

That afternoon, Jack Girick calls Bertha and Meyer aside.

*–Can you come to my office in half an hour? Don't be late.*

Bertha's pulse is racing, but her brother is his usual cheerful self. An ordinary half-hour drags by like snails on hot asphalt. The siblings walk close together and whisper to one another.

*–Do you reckon we've done something wrong?*

*–I don't know.*

*–Maybe someone wants to adopt us!*

*–I hope not.*

*–Well, what on earth could it be?*

They knock tentatively on Jack's door.

*–Come in, come in.*

Michael Sharlitt is waiting with Jack Girick and Bertha imagines that he looks at them fondly, with nostalgia even. *It's because we're going to be adopted*, she thinks furiously. *He's thinking of how he's going to break this to us.*

*–Would you two like some hot chocolate?*

*–Yes, please*, Meyer says. Bertha nods, her mouth dry. As she scans

the room for prospective parents, she imagines patronising, condescending faces. *Get on with it,* she wants to say. It's torture to wait.

Jack goes about making hot chocolate and motions the orphans to sit in leather-covered chairs.

*–Here you are. Take care, it's hot.*

Bertha nods her thanks and wraps her hands around the warm cup. She's certain now. Someone wants to adopt them. She can feel her brother's nervousness although nothing in his expression reveals it. She misses her mother. And then a rabbi appears in the doorway, his cheeks red, his beard long and black.

*–Bertha, Meyer, this is Rabbi Rabinowitz. He's the one responsible for getting you into our orphanage in the first place. He was in the area and thought he'd stop in to see how life is treating you both.*

This is the Taker. Bertha recognises the rabbi as the man who came to get them after their mother died.

*–Shalom,* says the rabbi. He shakes Meyer's hand. *And how are you liking it here?*

*–Pretty swell!*

*–And you, Bertha?*

*–Fine, thank you. It's very nice, thank you.*

*–Michael Sharlitt tells me that he's proud of your good behaviour and your good grades at school.*

*–Thank you,* Bertha says again. Joy is rising. They are not going to be adopted after all.

*–The children are very well,* Jack Girick confirms. *Bertha is a fine young lady, and Meyer is a champion at all kinds of sports, especially baseball. One of the finest boys in our care.*

And so the conversation continues for some minutes. The orphans finish their hot chocolate and are excused from the rabbi's presence. When they are out of sight and earshot, they hold hands and run towards the cottages, laughing, shrieking beneath the sapling trees, insane with joy. Meyer bumps his sister with his shoulder and she shoves him back hard, giggling.

–*I thought we were going to be adopted*, Meyer says.

–*Me too. But come to think of it, who wants half-grown children anyway? Kids who get adopted are babies. That way they can actually grow up thinking their adoptive parents are their parents.*

–*Yeah. This is my home and I'm never leaving.*

–*Me too. Well, until we have to.*

And so a certain affection for the orphan home, which was not there before, takes hold in Bertha's heart. She knows, with some vehemence now, that this is her place, and she doesn't want to be taken from it. That would be one loss too many, to have to leave her new family: Arleen, Gert, Al – even Michael Sharlitt, and the dragon cottage mother.

✡

Gert, Arleen and Bertha all turn fifteen in 1931 – the year that Al Capone is indicted and Robert Goddard patents the liquid-fuel rocket that will lead to a moon-landing in 1969. In less than seven years, Bertha's life will change forever.

But for now, it's the first half of 1931; Bert, Arleen and Gert listen to the radio broadcasts of *Little Orphan Annie* once a week in the dragon's own wing of the cottage. Gert smirks with derision afterwards.

–*Like hell it's like that. Yeah, sure, we're all one big happy family. Daddy Warbucks will save you all … what nonsense.*

–*We all wish it were true though.* Bertha states the obvious.

–*Oh, it's unfair, to say the least. Do you think whoever wrote that gave one single thought to what it might be like for real kids in real orphanages? I've a right to give them a piece of my mind.*

*–Okay, Gerty, don't listen anymore if you hate it so.*

*–Don't you tell me what to do, Queen Arleen. I've a right to listen, and a right to react.*

The event that divides the year is the Fourth of July fireworks at the Cleveland Stadium. As a special treat, the home kids are surprised with front-row seats and witness the city's first big fireworks display.

Bertha watches the blue and green stars bursting overhead and blocks her ears against the explosions. The enormity of everything out there hits her like a wave. Her throat feels tight, but her eyes stay dry.

Going to the pictures in summer is all about which boys will be there, and who will say what, and who will wear what. Charlie Chaplin's *City Lights* lifts them out of their orphanage existence with a new kind of laughter. The little man with big shoes wins their hearts and they can't get enough of him. He's the underdog, misunderstood by everyone, it seems, except for the adoring orphans who will him to triumph and who understand every nuance, every twitch of his funny moustache.

One Saturday morning, Meyer is off with the baseball team to watch a professional game. (Since he actually got to go see the unbelievable Babe Ruth himself some weeks back, he talks about nothing else.) Al is torn between wanting to join his buddies and spending the afternoon sitting next to Bert, laughing for ninety minutes. He chooses the latter.

*–Did you see the new Empire State Building pictures? It's the most awesome thing,* Al whispers to Bertha. *Don't you just love living in America? I do.*

*–Hush up, will you please?* Arleen says across Bertha's chest. *I'm concentrating on the picture in front of me, if you don't mind.*

*–D'you believe them Scottsboro boys are guilty or innocent?* Al continues in lower tones. *I don't know what to think. It's a terrible thought, but if they didn't rape those two women, then a bunch of innocent kids are all gonna die.*

*–Al, would you please shush? Bertha here is trying to watch a funny show and you're spoiling it.* Gert's voice crests over all the heads in her row.

Bertha feels Al shrink beside her. She leans over, her dark blonde curls falling over her face so he can't see her expression, and she whispers, *We'll talk after, okay?*

And after the film, as Gert and Arleen are making their way out, Al grabs Bert's good hand and hangs on to it.

*–Do you want to go steady?* he asks her breathlessly, seizing what he knows will be a rare moment of privacy. The air between them is taut with hope.

Bertha sees the flash of fear and longing in his eyes. His fair hair is unruly and his face has transformed into planes and angles over the past year and a half.

*–Y'see, Bert, I'm crazy about you. I would do anything for you. You are everything to me and always will be.*

She's shaking but she puts her crippled hand over his and pats it in a sisterly way.

*–Al, you're my pal. I can't go steady with you. You're like a brother to me. I care for you in that way.*

*–Oh gee,* he says. He drops her hand and takes in a big ragged breath. *Are you mad at me?*

*–Of course not. But I can't go with you. For one, I'm older than you, and two, you're my brother's best friend, and three, I just don't care for you in … in the way … you know. Al, you'll always be my pal, okay? I'm not everything to you and nor should you say that. Think of me as your home sister, 'cause that's what I am.*

At this point, Gert and Arleen poke their heads back into the cinema and Gert's slightly envious voice cuts through to Al and Bert.

*–C'mon, you two. What's taking you so doggone long?*

Gert's advice to Bert during confirmation cooking class is to re-think Al's proposal.

*–He's going to be good-looking, and all the girls will be falling for him. Is it his skin? They grow out of that, you know. I mean, look at your brother, he's all pimply too, but it's not like it's gonna last.*

*–No, Gerty, it's not his skin! I've said it a hundred times. He's like a brother to me. If you like him so much, why don't you go with him?*

*–Well, if I could! But he didn't ask me, and I guess that would be sort of shameful to be someone's second choice. Now go get the sugar or this pie won't happen.*

In the large pantry cupboard, Bertha listens to the girls chattering away. Confirmation and almost-adulthood are just months away. And then what? She can't imagine life beyond the orphanage. All the excitement doesn't move her one bit. She doesn't want to be away from Meyer. The Opportunity Home for Girls has been the choice for many other grads, but it's had some bad stories coming from it. The word is, it's supposed to be a place where home girls can find employment in the art of making clothes and other tasks, but from what she's heard, it seems to be more about the managers having the opportunity to take advantage of cheap labour, and that isn't what she wants for herself.

*–Bert, what are you doing in that cupboard for so long?*

She grabs a heavy bag of sugar and hauls it out to the long table, putting it down in front of Gert. *I couldn't find the sugar.*

*–Wow! That's pretty white. I thought the sugar was more browny … sort of.*

*–Let's get to work, Gerty. This pie's already way behind.*

The girls wait with anticipation as the fruit pies bake and the smell stirs their stomachs and imaginations.

*–I swear I'm gonna bake pies every single day for lunch when I have my own life*, Gert says.

*–Maybe pies won't seem so important to you then.*

*–Yeah, I know. It'll probably be boys. Or both.*

When the pies are ready, the girls can barely hold in their desperation to cut into the hot pastry and test their creative efforts. Gert lifts a forkful to her mouth. Then she runs like the devil to the trash and spits out the pie. Bertha's fork is mid-air.

*–What's the matter with you, Gerty?*

*–With me? With me? It was salt you hauled from the pantry, Bertha! You donkey, you!*

A moment passes, one that Bertha almost recognises as anguish. And then Gert laughs, and she laughs, and Mrs Goldberg, the overlord of the confirmation cooking class, tells them to shush, please.

Bert and Gert exchange looks of complicity, and as the other girls finish their pies, the two go around the room generously offering salty slices to any girls who feel they've not yet had sufficient to suffice.

✡

Cold weather always seems to arrive quickly. It's as though the earth suddenly falls and tilts away from the sun. One morning it's warm and muggy, and then the next, it's darker, colder, at the very same time of day. Chores before school seem to take so much longer. The air is filled with the smell of decomposing leaves. Gert loves the change of season, but Bertha remarks that it reeks of decay and she sees no beauty in the encroaching dark days. Fall has arrived, crisping the grass with frost, making clouds of white in front of the schoolkids waiting for the bus outside Heights High.

*–Hi, Bert.*

*–Hi, Al.*

*–You cold?*

*–Always.*

*–Here, you can have my jacket.*

*–No, really.*

*–C'mon, don't be silly. I'm not even cold.*

*–Okay, thanks.*

Al lets her go first into the bus and then follows her to her seat.

*–Mind if I do?*

*–No, of course not.*

He sits down next to her, and she sneaks a sideways glance at him. Gert's right. In the past few months, his skin has cleared. His jaw is heavier, and his whole body has suddenly filled out.

Al's leg presses against hers. As the bus starts, he reaches out and takes her hand, the misshapen one, discreetly in his. No one can see anything but two young people staring straight ahead.

*–You're icy,* he says. She doesn't take her hand away. He continues to look straight ahead and clears his throat. His grasp is confident, firm, older. They sit like that until they're five minutes from the home.

Al drops his voice so it's almost a whisper.

*–I'll be honest. It's taken me weeks to get to this moment with enough guts, and it might not happen again … and I don't wanna lose my self-respect by asking you embarrassing questions again. I know you think of me as your kid brother's friend, and it may not ever be any different. But Bert, you are, and always will be, the girl of my dreams. As long as I live, I'll carry a torch for you.*

Bertha's cheeks are on fire. Her hands twitch away from his, not because she doesn't like the shape of his fingers over hers, but because the emotions that come swirling out of nowhere are so foreign and unintelligible that she fears she might faint.

He lets go, and she gets up as the bus comes to a stop. She holds on to the chair for support and then mumbles as she shrugs out of his coat. No one must see that she hands it back to him. She drops it on the seat and dares not meet his eyes, though she feels his stare.

*–Thanks, Al. I'm fine now. See you later.*

She bustles through the crowd of teenagers and runs until she catches up with Gert and Arleen.

*–I didn't even see you on the bus. I was looking for you!*

*–She was sitting next to Al. I told you, Gerty,* Arleen says.

*–Hey girls, Friday night. Feinkuchen treat and singsong!* Bertha says, and pushes her renegade emotions into the pit of her stomach.

In the days leading up to confirmation, the strains of Handel's *Largo*, played on the pipe organ by Miss Schaffer, who also leads the choir, drift from the chapel. The final exam at Hebrew school is done, and Bertha, Arleen and Gert rush excitedly to the wardrobe to try on the dresses and corsages that will turn them into movie-star versions of themselves. Only, they have to face another dragon. The Irish wardrobe mistress, Miss Rose Ward (is that her real name, they wonder), is going to be either sugary sweet or stark raving mad.

Luck is on their side. Miss Ward is having a good day, and her cheer is infectious as she pulls and pushes the girls first into the right position, and then into the right clothes.

*–I can't wait for my wedding day,* Gert announces, smoothing the silky cotton material over her legs.

*–That could be some time away,* Bertha says. *Live for the moment.*

*–Say, Bert, I think living for the future is what keeps me going.*

*–What's happening after confirmation?*

*–A trip to town.* Two *shows ... dinner between the first and the second. And bedtime postponed until eleven pm!*

*–I feel like a real hick.* Gert is bubbling with excitement. *Did I ever mention my philosophy? Every dog has his day, and ours is almost here, ladies.*

This confirmation day is for the class of 1932. Handel's *Largo* begins with the 32-foot organ pipes responding to the light touch of Miss Schaffer's fingers on the keyboard. The notes of the aria rise majestically to the top of the chapel, layers of measured beauty that say what words cannot. The confirmation boys are wearing black serge suits and Bertha is one of the white angels standing next to them.

Behind her, sitting at the back of the chapel, is Jacob Frank.

His foot keeps time with each new tier of harmony. The high flute-pipes take over the melody and, as the swell opens, the bass notes resonate beneath the floor and travel through each body in the room, changing cellular structure, changing history. The music of the Jewish-born Lutheran carries the group of orphans from childhood into adulthood and deposits them on the doorstep of life.

In 1932, Bertha Frank is sixteen years old, and her whole life lies ahead of her, an unmarked page of possibility.

✡

From the future of such a narrative you can look back and see beyond the lives of the characters; you know their futures and see the results of their choices. You see how the story flows like a river, finding the faultlines, the soft places in the territory of the soul to carve out its passage. When I am eleven, I do not understand why the sound of the violin stirs my blood and causes an aching within my chest. I do not know why the German lessons at school in South Africa seem so easy, or why I begin to repeat the words with such precision that no accent is detectable.

✡

Chicago. City of wind and sky-scraping buildings. Bertha can hardly believe she is out in the world now. Jack Girick has told her not to fret: this is just a visit. Perhaps they will offer to take her in, but for all intents and purposes she needs to remember that there is no pressure from anyone. The home will always help her out. Aunt Helen and Aunt Saidie live on the tenth floor in an apartment on the South Side of Chicago. This is her destination – the home of Jacob's sisters.

Bertha gets off the train and takes a taxi to the given address. Her senses are reeling. The trees have been stripped naked by the wind, and there is the salty tang of Lake Michigan. She stands outside the grey building, looking up.

She doesn't even know if she wants to be taken in by an aunt, or a cousin.

Her insecurity follows her inside and up the elevator to the door of apartment 1064. She knocks.

When he opens the door, she does not recognise him at first. She wasn't expecting him to be there; she thought he was working. And by the lines on his face and the loose skin beneath his eyes, she marks how time has passed. The smell of onions and oil hangs over him.

–*Dad?*

–*My daughter*, he says, in English. He does not hug her, but leans over and places a fleeting kiss on top of her head.

He looks over his shoulder and says in Yiddish, זי איז דאָ! *She's here!*

A heavy-set woman wearing an apron waddles up behind Jacob.

–*Hello, Bertha. I'm Aunty Saidie. Your father, he speaks still so little English. Do you still speak Yiddish?*

–*No, Aunty Saidie. I forgot it all.*

*–Well, it is a pity. You cannot even speak to your own father! Here, put your coat on the stand. Come and sit down and talk with your Aunty Helen. She is not so good at English.*

Jacob perches on the edge of the sagging couch. His sister bangs around in the kitchen. He tries to make conversation. He gestures at the apartment furnishings – the plum-coloured curtains, the stained rug on the ground. *Nice*, he says.

*–Yeah, I guess it is nice*, Bertha says. *I wasn't expecting to see you, Dad. It's good to see you.*

*–Yes. Meyer?*

*–He's doing very well.*

Aunt Helen nods her greeting to Bertha.

*–My English is not perfect*, she says. *You like kneidlach soup? It's not Pesach, but kneidlach is good for the cold weather.*

Eventually, all the food is on the table. Bertha looks across at her father and her two aunts. She has become a stranger. She does not see herself in their coarse features. Her father's hands tremble slightly as he holds his soup spoon to his lips. Perhaps she is there, she thinks, in the shape of his fingernails. When he looks up for a moment, something like the eruption of long-buried grief streaks across his eyes and forehead, but then he focuses on the explicit task of carving his matzo ball in half with a soup spoon.

And when Bertha leaves for the long train journey back to Cleveland in the late afternoon, she senses that the door to a new life in Chicago is not about to open.

She does not hear from Jacob, or from either of her aunts. Eventually Michael Sharlitt calls her into his office.

*–Mr Sharlitt?*

Perhaps she has grown up overnight, but she suddenly cannot imagine how Michael Sharlitt ever made her afraid. That forbidding glare is nothing but a veneer over a soft heart, which for decades has held close the welfare of hundreds of children like her. And then she looks away.

–*Bertha. Have a seat.* He sucks on his pipe and trips over his dog. *Schatz, will you get out of the way, or are you trying to kill me?* He scoots the sausage dog under a chair with his foot.

–*Well, I sent several letters to your aunts and even to your cousins, requesting they consider taking you in. Today I received this note.*

He walks over to Bertha, his brow furrowed with the exertion of drawing in as much smoke from his pipe as he can, and shows her the uneven handwriting. She reads: … *times are hard and we cannot afford to take Bertha in.*

And so Bertha finds herself moving to the other side of Cleveland to a foster home. At first she believes she will be able to complete her schooling, but it soon becomes obvious that this family thinks no such thing.

Mrs Levy raps on her bedroom door and wakes Bertha every morning at six am.

–*You're a lazy girl, Bertha! How am I ever going to get things done if you aren't in the kitchen already?*

–*It's six in the morning. I'm not late!*

–*Don't you talk back, young lady. I'm doing you a favour taking you in like this, and don't you forget it. Now, Ari needs his porridge, and after that, you'll mop the floor, clean the dishes and make sure Ari goes down for a nap at ten. You can start lunch while he's sleeping. Oh, and Mr Levy is having his boss for dinner tonight, so I want you to prepare the chicken for me. Hurry up, will you?*

Bertha struggles through the year. She becomes so insolent that the family threatens to contact Michael Sharlitt and ask for her to be removed from their home. Bertha beats them to it and contacts him herself: *Please, Mr Sharlitt. I need to move to another home as this one has become impossible.*

She is taken in by a new family in which she becomes privy to the meaning of a word she has learned: dysfunction. She loses eight pounds. Her back aches. Her eyes smart from exhaustion. Soon, she is ready to run away.

On a summer afternoon when the temperature has topped a hundred degrees and sweat rushes down her back, she packs all her worldly possessions into a carry-bag and, using her meagre allowance, catches a taxi back to Bellefaire.

Michael Sharlitt's office is a welcome sight. Bertha is so happy to see him she wants to throw her arms around him, but that would not be proper. She sits anxiously in a familiar leather chair and drums her good fingers on the upholstered arm.

*–I'm glad to see you, Bertha. I hear you've come on some hard times again?*

*–I'm sorry to report, Mr Sharlitt, that the latest foster home is not working well for me. I'm very unhappy there and I can't bear to stay another night. I hoped at first I might get to finish my last two years of school, but I gave that up ages ago.*

He peers out at her from hooded brows, reaches over his desk and pulls his pipe out of the top drawer. Schatz gets up off the floor when he smells the pungent smoke, and goes to sit at Bertha's feet. Bertha is trembling inside, but it's a kind of fury. The fury is widespread and its targets include her aunts, cousins and everybody who wouldn't have her, who turned their backs on two children right from the beginning because not a single relative had the capacity or the desire to take on extra mouths to feed.

*–Mr Sharlitt, this is the worst place yet. The first place was miserable: the mother hated me and said terrible things to me all day. But*

*I could still hold my head up. Now, in this house, the people are sick, Mr Sharlitt. They make me sleep in a baby's cot. In a crib. I have constant headaches from lying curled up in a box all night. I'm not one to complain, but this is my last resort coming back here. I have nowhere to go.*

She can feel her cheeks are red. She contains herself, but inside, a river has burst its banks. How dare anyone treat a human being in this way? She hears her father's voice from long ago whispering stories about cruelty and oppression, stories that lie buried in the dream of early childhood. Life is like this because she has no mother, and no family to take her in.

*–Bertha, just wait here a minute, will you? I will return shortly.*

He exits in a plume of cigar smoke and Schatz moves his short legs over her feet, hemming her in so that she's forced to stroke his soft fur and pointy snout.

When the door opens again, Bertha stares into the smiling face of Jack Girick. He takes her hand and shakes it warmly. He seems smaller than before, she thinks as he pulls up a chair in front of her. He reports all Meyer's successes and then assures her that her brother will be waiting to see her for lunch in thirty minutes. Michael Sharlitt re-enters his office and blows smoke rings at the window.

Jack Girick's words are like home. They pull her back to normality.

*–And so, you've written to all your relatives again?*

*–I wrote to everyone in this country.*

*–No one could offer you a place?*

She shakes her head and looks at her hands.

*–They have busy lives. Full houses. No room. No money.*

*–Have you told your father?*

She shakes her head again. She's sure he knows. *Meyer says he's looking for work himself at the moment. It would break his heart.*

*–Does he write?*

*–Occasionally.*

*–And Meyer surely knows your situation?*

She nods.

*–Are you in touch with other friends from the home?*

*–Gertrude and I are. She lives with her sisters not too far from here. Oh, I hear from Arleen too, and Al, who's determined he's going to be a doctor.*

*–Would that be Gert Fogelson?*

*–Yes.*

*–Bertha, my dear, just leave it with me. Go and find Meyer. He should be outside the Alumnus Hall. Go into town with him and have lunch. Come back here in the afternoon, and I will have a plan for you.*

Michael Sharlitt, who has been quietly sucking everything in through his pipe, surveys Bertha and Schatz. He says, *We will always be here for you, my dear. If things don't work out, we are your home and your family. You can depend on that.*

Bertha stands and blinks hard. Tears burn but do not fall.

*–Thank you. Thank you very much.*

Bellefaire is as she left it. The chapel with its basement classrooms sits on top of the lawn like a friendly animal. The woods, the playing fields and the volleyball court are all unchanged.

It is she who has changed. Without the guidance of parents, the world is a sea of sucking tides that can pull and push a soft soul in any direction. What doesn't kill you makes you stronger, says Gert. By that same token, Bertha thinks, what doesn't make you stronger kills you. She knows this.

When she sees Meyer, the entire burden of the past eighteen months dissolves. His hair is thick and red-gold. He's tall and athletic.

His eyes dance with laughter and he opens his arms. She runs across the lawn and throws herself at her brother, almost knocking him to the ground. He picks her up and spins her around.

They walk arm in arm into the sunshine, letting go of each other only to pay for the bus and to sit down for a nickel hamburger at Nobby's Hamburger Joint, where they eat for old times' sake, and imagine what they might do in the future.

*–You just need to be on your own for another nine months. Then, as soon as I graduate, we'll get somewhere together, I promise.*

*–We'll need jobs.*

*–We'll get jobs. Say, have you written to Uncle Woolf and Aunty Dora in South Africa?*

*–No.*

*–Well?*

*–What should I say?*

*–Just ask them how they are … and the cousins. Send them your confirmation picture too. You're as pretty as a picture, Bert, and twice as smart as anyone else I know. I wish Helen had half as much good sense as you. She'd choose me then!*

*–Who's Helen?*

*–Gal I met at school. I've fallen for her pretty hard, but it seems the feelings are not mutual.*

Bertha laughs for the first time in months. By the end of the afternoon, the siblings are full of hope. When they return to the administration building, Michael Sharlitt has lost the frown on his forehead, and Jack Girick beams as he informs the two of them that Gert's older sister Lenore would be only too happy to share the apartment that she and Gert and one other sister live in, in exchange for some housekeeping once a week, *just*, Jack adds with raised finger and eyebrow, so that she may feel neither *guilt* nor *liability* for accepting an offer of room and board. He fails to mention the additional money that he, under instruction from Michael Sharlitt, has offered to pay for Bertha's room and board until she finds employment.

Life with the Fogelsons is mostly a welcome relief. Gert is euphoric to have her dearest friend in the same house. Lenore works hard to appear gracious to the girls. She even finds them jobs at a chocolate factory. The work is 'piece work', paid by the number of small chocolates a person can wrap in an hour.

Bertha battles to hold the chocolates and wrap them with her deformed hand. They slip from her grasp and she's ashamed of how her finished pieces look. She cannot complete anything fast enough to keep the job. She leaves work in tears after a week.

Thankfully, she finds another job, at the May Company Department Store. At first she spends almost the entire day in the dusty, dirty stockroom. But sales are also part of the job, and as her co-workers and supervisors begin to take note of her engaging smile, her laughing blue eyes and sandy golden curls, and her meticulous managing of the cash, she is sent less and less to the stockroom. Soon, Bertha becomes the star of May's clothing department.

At home, fleeting shadows darken the brightness of her day.

There isn't enough to eat.

It seems that everyone gets more than Bertha at mealtimes. Sometimes Lenore is in a bad mood. Frequently, Bertha feels like a burden, the intruder in a tightly knit family, regardless of how close she and Gertrude can be.

–*You sure could do with a bit of fat on your bones*, Gert says enviously as they get ready to go out. *You'd better not make Don fall in love with you. I have my eye on him.*

–*I'll do my best, Gertie. But Don can like whomever he likes, can't he?*

–*You saying you like him?*

*–I might!*

*–You're driving me crazy, Bert!*

*–Well, he bought tickets for the both of us, you* and *me, to the Mayfair Casino, didn't he?*

*–I plan to dance with him all night.*

*–Good luck!*

In the cocktail lounge at the Mayfair Casino, an Art Deco supper club in the former Ohio Theatre, Bertha has no idea how many heads turn her way. But Gert sees it. Despite her loyalty towards her friend, the pain of envy proves overwhelming. She goes out of her way to compete, and when it appears that the handsome Don is falling for Bertha's winning smile, Gert prances up to them with two drinks, one in each hand.

*–Could you just hold these for a moment, Bert?*

Bertha's smile falters. She keeps one hand firmly behind her back.

*–Oh, do stop being so fussed about your hand. C'mon, Bert!*

Don's attention is drawn to Bertha's hand. She flushes in the crimson light. She reaches out both hands, takes the drinks and holds them mid-air for a moment. Her eyes are cold. In the startled look that crosses Don's face for a fraction of a second, she sees his horror. She places the glasses on the floor at his feet and turns her head, tossing her thick hair, and glides out of the room, out of the theatre, into the hot summer night.

✡

Years later, when Bertha is living an unimaginable life on a foreign continent, Gertrude will think back on some of the things that transpired, and tell Bert how she never meant any harm, how she feels bad, in retrospect. How, without parents to guide them, the orphans had to do the best they could with what they had.

A door to Bertha's soul has quietly closed. She realises she is utterly alone in the world.

At night she cries for her mother.

Some weeks later, Saturdays regain their exceptional status. It's as if the night at the Mayfair Casino never happened. Gert is full of jokes again, and her envy seems to have evaporated. There are good times to be had shopping, going to the pictures and meeting eligible young men. These subjects are worthy of late-night discussion and Bertha enjoys sitting at the foot of Gert's bed, listening to outlandish tales and telling some herself.

Bertha becomes more aware of the effect she has on men. She is neither blind nor indifferent to the attention they pay her. But she's looking for something that none of these men appear to offer, and she doesn't know where she will find it.

At Meyer's urging, Bertha finally sends a letter to her Uncle Woolf in South Africa – an act that will change the direction of the river of time. She includes a photograph of herself in a white dress, standing with her brother and her father. Her hands are clasped behind her back so that her fingers do not show. She asks after her Uncle Woolf's and Aunty Dora's good health and informs them that she is eighteen and recently moved out from foster care, and living with her best friend, Gertrude Fogelson. She tells them that Meyer is a champion athlete, that he is soon to be confirmed and will graduate with the class of 1935, before expressing her hopes of hearing from her mother's brother.

Some months later, she receives a reply from her Uncle Woolf and Aunt Dora: they are so pleased she has written. She looks beautiful – the image of her mother. There is news about her cousins, one of them named Mildred and around her age, and a snap of the whole family. They look forward to hearing from her again.

When Meyer graduates, he takes a room with the Fogelsons, and there is envy in the household because Bertha and Meyer are twin souls. In the evenings, Gert no longer has Bertha to herself. Brother and sister seem drawn into one another's orbit the minute they see each other after work. Bertha is delighted when she walks in the door and sees Meyer writing letters or making dinner. But she has to make a concerted effort to give Gert the requisite attention so that her friend does not feel she's being left out.

At the apartment in 1517 East Boulevard, Cleveland, Ohio, Bertha and Meyer finally feel at home. They bicker. They laugh together. They dream of what they might be. In the months that go by, they send small gifts and cards to their father and to Michael Sharlitt and Jack Girick, wishing them mazel tov for their birthdays.

It's the Jewish New Year and Gert complains that Bertha gets all the mail that ever comes to their address. Bertha has received from her father a card that she will treasure for the rest of her life. The card will be kept safe through time and movement across three continents. Almost eighty years after it is written, Jacob's great-granddaughter will hold the card in her hands, next to her heart.

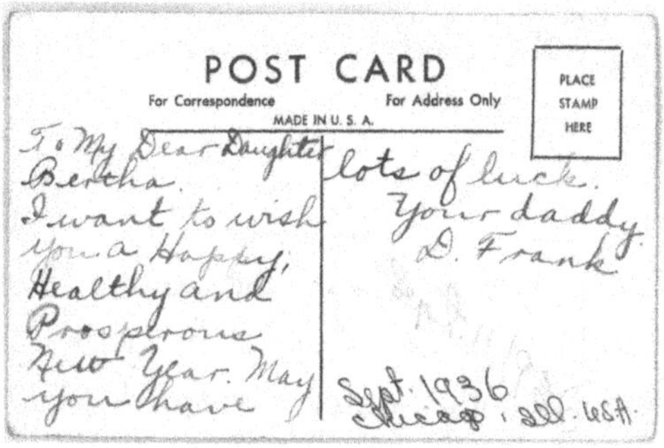

✡

Jacob sits in his one-room apartment in Chicago, watching the snow fall outside. His children are grown and he does not know them. He feels he has failed in a colossal sense: he has heard, only recently, about his daughter being shunted from foster home to foster home, about her being mistreated. Sleeping in a cot. Scrubbing floors. He buries his face in his hands. He was unable to protect her. And he still can't. He has not a cent to his name. He will call in on Sam Epstein, whose little boy has a talent for the violin. He will surely get some teaching. Apart from that, his only hope is that Lakeview Apartments will contact him and offer him the nightwatchman position. He still can't sleep properly, so this job seems like the most fitting position for him: he will be the guardian of the night while others sleep.

Life must not crush his daughter's spirit. It cannot happen.

The words he writes to his daughter in September 1936 are the oldest words his great-granddaughter inherits – and therefore infinitely precious. They belie the enormous world of grief and hope beneath them. She will know that English cannot make his world visible. And she will understand that he placed his children in the care of Michael Sharlitt because of love: that he wished, with all his heart, that their lives might not follow a tragic curve.

✡

The girl who gives up the violin at eleven thinks the music dies in her, but it doesn't. Like a river that vanishes underground carrying the secret of its source, currents that had their origins in distant times and places sometimes bubble to the surface. They are not immediately recognisable as being part of the hidden river. They emerge in other places, like the ability to speak certain languages without an accent. First she is immersed in Afrikaans, the language of the ruling party in South Africa: *Goeie more mense, dis 'n lekker dag vandag.* Then she devours German, which the children learn at school too: *Diese Sprache hört sich sehr vertraut an. Ich spreche fast ohne Akzent.* The German teacher is convinced that the girl must have German parents, but of course she doesn't. She also loves Zulu, the main African language in the highveld, and taught at school by Mama Gladys, who, as a black Zulu teacher, is an anomaly in the apartheid republic. *Siyabonga Abazali, ufunda isiZulu.* The Zulu teacher takes the girl's small white hands in her dark ones and stares into her eyes, saying, *Woza lapa, Sisi, I will tell you your future: you will travel far away, on planes, and talk to many people in foreign lands. You will tell them some important things, I think.*

✡

In the spring of 1937, the year that Bertha turns twenty, she arrives home in the evening to find Meyer sitting on his chair, his wool-socked feet pressing against the radiator.

*–Letter for you, Bert. From South Africa. Someone Davidow as the sender. Look.*

Bertha hangs up her coat, slowly, deliberately. She feels a tug of excitement: something unknown, unexpected. A rare thing. She takes her time, gets something to drink from the fridge, fills a kettle with water and puts it on the stove.

*–Tea, Meyer?*

*–Sure, thanks. When are you going to open that letter?*

*–In a minute. What are you in such a hurry for?*

*–I want to know who it's from, that's what! And I bet you do too.*

*–All right, all right. You make the tea. I'll open the letter.*

Bertha takes a butter knife from a drawer and slowly slits open the pale blue envelope. Then she slides out the letter. It's four pages long, written in elegant slanting hand on pale blue paper.

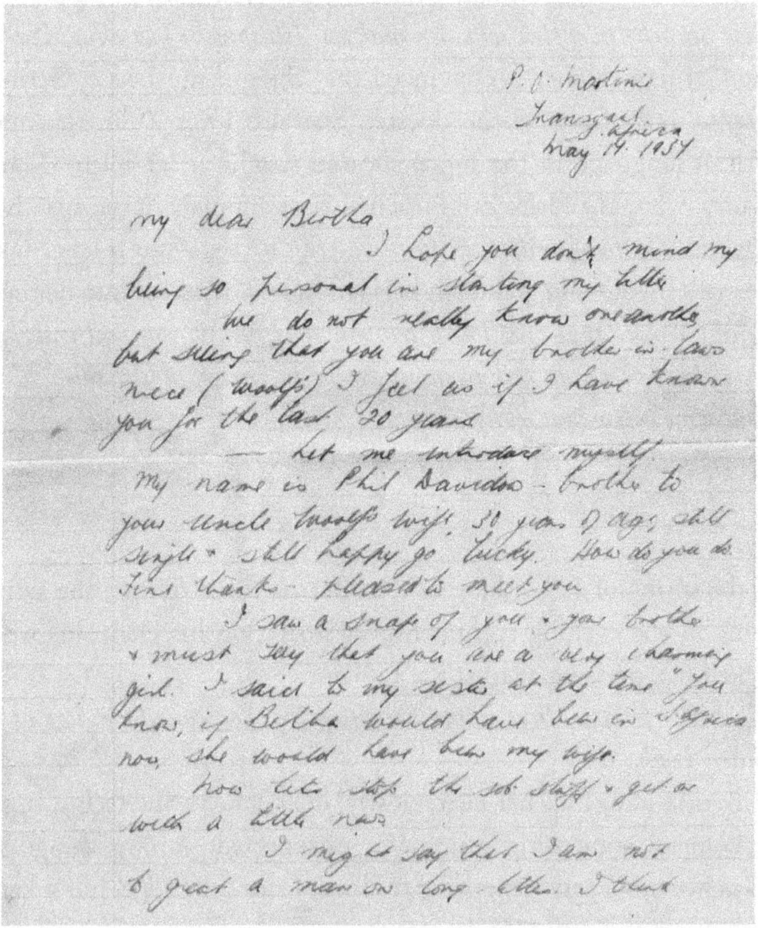
P.O. Martini
Transvaal
S. Africa
May 14. 1954

My dear Bertha
I hope you don't mind my being so personal in starting my letter. We do not really know one another, but seeing that you are my brother-in-law's niece (Woolf's) I feel as if I have known you for the last 20 years.
— Let me introduce myself.
My name is Phil Davidow - brother to your Uncle Woolf's wife. 30 years of age, still single & still happy go lucky. How do you do. Fine thanks - pleased to meet you.
I saw a snap of you & your brother & must say that you are a very charming girl. I said to my sister at the time "You know, if Bertha would have been in S. Africa now, she would have been my wife.
Now lets stop the sob stuff & get on with a little news.
I might say that I am not so great a man on long letters. I think



If not for this letter, the girl with the violin would not exist. The lives lived out in southern Africa would never have been. With the arrival of the letter, destinies will unfold far away from the small apartment in the Midwestern United States of America.

✡

P.O. Martini
Transvaal
S. Africa

May 17, 1937

My dear Bertha,

I hope you don't mind my being so personal in starting my letter.

We do not really know one another, but seeing that you are my brother-in-law's niece (Woolf's) I feel as if I have known you for the last 20 years.

Let me introduce myself. My name is Phil Davidow – brother to your Uncle Woolf's wife, 30 years of age, still single and still happy go lucky. How do you do. Fine thanks – pleased to meet you.

I saw a snap of you and your brother and must say you are a very charming girl ...

*–Well, come on, tell me, who's it from?*

*–Just a minute, Meyer. I have to read this.*

*–Your tea's ready.*

*–Not now, please!*

*–Okay, okay, don't be snappy. Just curious, is all.*

She re-reads the lines: *I said to my sister at the time, 'You know if Bertha would have been in S. Africa now, she would have been my wife.'* Her head spins. She re-reads another line: *I must say, you are a very charming girl.*

Her face is burning.

Phil gives her the details of young lives lived on a distant continent: two cousins are around her age, at university, and the two younger girls are still in high school. She can't stop reading:

I suppose you want to hear something about myself ... When I finished my schooling I was supposed to take up Law. I did so for 4 years and gave it up as a bad job. I then took up Chemistry and also gave it up as a bad job as it didn't interest me in the least. I then decided to go into the country. I have been here for the last 8 years and am quite satisfied with events as they have turned out.

I am partners with your uncle and we hit it off very well together. We have 3 stores and are busy opening our 4th one at the end of June. We are quite comfortable out here.

The place we are in is called the bushveld. It is miles from the nearest town. You must not think that by saying it's miles from town that it must be a terrible place. It is just the opposite. It is a thickly populated settlement and when the government are finished with the big irrigation scheme now in hand, there will be hundreds of families out here.

We are situated in a place where we get the sunshine practically 365 days in the year. It seems hard to believe, but it is so. Our summers are as warm and hot as can be expected, and our coldest winter days, which last about 1 month of the year, are as warm as your summer days.

I think my biggest worry and trouble is with my mother. She keeps on worrying me about getting married. I told her that I haven't as yet met the right girl. Now that I have seen a snap of her, I find that she is far off in America and by the time she gets this letter she will either be engaged or married.

I think that if she isn't, you will have to try and help me. What about it, Bertha. I never did believe in love at first sight but now I do.

Bertha struggles to believe what she is reading. It's as if he knows her, understands her, or, at least, knows how to get her to understand him.

If you write me every week, I will reply to you immediately. I would like to write every week, but do not know how you will receive this letter. I think I have written enough for the time being.

Fond love from Uncle Woolf, Aunt Dora and their family.

Please reply soon and remember,

Yours,
Phil

*–So, Bert, what does it say?*

*–It's from Phil Davidow. Uncle Woolf's partner and brother-in-law. Wait. I have to read something again. It's hard to read.*

Bertha holds the page to the light and fixates on his even writing, trying to imagine the person who makes these words. She knows her face is red.

*–Now you're hiding something. Go on, tell me.*

*–All right then. It's a love letter, Meyer.*

Bertha is cautious when she writes back to Phil. She describes her and Meyer's life. She sends her love to Phil's sister Dora (her aunt) and to her Uncle Woolf, her mother's brother. Her mother's brother! It is as if she's never contemplated this before: Woolf's blood is the same as her mother's. They had the same parents. He creeps into her heart and stays there as she writes to Phil. She knows her questions are naïve but she has no choice. So, she asks about Africa. What is it like? Is it civilised or do wild animals roam the towns? She asks Phil to send her some pictures, if he can. Then she writes letters to each of her cousins, and to her aunt and uncle. She mails those first, re-reads her letter to Phil, and then sends it on to him.

One summer evening, when she returns from work, sweaty and grumpy and having just turned down an invitation to go to the pictures with Gert and Arleen, Meyer is sitting at home in his chair, waving a pale pink envelope at her. She reaches for it, her heart racing, and he holds it high over her head.

–*Give me that!*

–*Come and get it!* Meyer gets up and dashes first into the bathroom, then into his bedroom, then into hers, and, finally, back into the living room. He's laughing and Bertha wants to strangle him, though she's laughing too.

–*Quit teasing me! It's undignified to have to chase your own brother around the apartment to get what is rightfully your own letter.*

–*You can't be that crazy about him, Bert.*

–*Give me the letter, Meyer! I have to have it!*

–*All right, all right. Just having a bit of fun.*

Bertha grabs the envelope. This time, to Meyer's disappointment, she disappears into her room to read the letter alone. It is dated August 4, 1937.

My dear Bertha

Very many thanks for your most eagerly awaited-for letter. You know, I started giving up hope of ever receiving a reply from you. All my nieces had already received a reply and I was the last one …

What can I say about myself. As I wrote before, I told you my approximate age. I am 5ft 8" in height, brown eyes (at least I think so), medium colour hair and still a bachelor. I am supposed to be a bit old-fashioned in my ideas. You know, I really can't give a description of myself because I am not used to flattery or anything of that line.

I very much wanted to enclose a snap of myself … but promise you one in my next letter to you, even if taken last year together with a friend of mine while I was down at the Cape on a round South Africa tour in my car.

I have been in this district now for 8 years and feel quite at home out here, although I was brought up in a city – Johannesburg – and worked there after leaving high-school …

I have always been of a quiet type of person and never did feel inclined to mix with other people, that is why I actually left Johannesburg for the country.

I have also roughed it a lot. I was all on my own for 3 years in a small Land Store of your uncle Woolf's when he was patrons with another person. He broke away after that and we both joined hands and have been together since then …

Listen, Bertha, wouldn't you give the idea of settling down in this country of ours a good thought. I know that you will say that you think you will find it hard to adapt yourself to this country and that you can't leave your brother alone. Well, the two of you could come out. It wouldn't cost either of you a penny or cent as they say in America.

You might think it funny me asking you as I have never seen you before, but honestly, as soon as I saw your snap I told my sister that if you were anywhere in S. Africa, I would soon get in touch with you and see what I could do for myself.

I am getting older instead of younger and my mum would like me to settle down … I know you might think it hard to leave your relatives, but if you do come, you will still be coming to an uncle who will be waiting with open arms. Not only your uncle would be waiting but also I would be waiting.

Please give this matter an honest thought. I know I am asking you to do a very big thing, but I can promise you that you will never regret it.

Bertha dear, I hope there is no one else that can keep you back, let me play on your sentiment and ask you to come here and make me happy. It is a big undertaking, but you won't regret it.

I will be looking forward to your reply with Anxiety. I have never approached anyone yet on a matter like this. I know what I am asking you and quite realise what it is, but please say yes in your reply. It will make me the happiest man in this world. If I had my way, I would come over and take you according to caveman ideas, but that wouldn't do.

Remember that although we are thousands of miles apart, you can still make someone in this world walk on air by only saying one small word – yes.

I will now conclude with best love from all out here.

May I conclude with tons of love,

Yours,
Phil

Bertha's soul is on fire. She feels she might faint. Did he write that? *If I had my way I would come over and take you according to caveman ideas, but that wouldn't do.*

No, it certainly wouldn't! She knows her face is as red as a freshly cut beetroot. She laughs out loud, and then wants to cry. By the time Meyer enters the room she has contained herself as best she can. When he looks questioningly at his sister's blotched complexion, he knows something is up.

*–He wants me to go to South Africa, Meyer. He'll pay for everything. And he wants you to come too, if you like.*

✡

12.8.37

Dear Bertha,

This will not exactly be a letter in any shape or form.

It is just a … note with the snaps I am sending, also some postcards of Johannesburg.

As you will see, we are quite civilised.

Please don't take any notice of the clothes I am wearing in those snaps as they were taken on my tour around S. Africa by car. I am standing alone in one of the snaps and am the shorter of the two in the other.

They are just rough snaps, but as soon as I get a decent one, I will certainly post it on to you.

As I said before, this is not a letter, so I will conclude by sending tons of love from all here.

The sooner I get a letter from you, the sooner I will be a happier man.

Good night little girl,

Tons of love,
Phil

Bertha's breathing is shallow. She picks up the two snaps and looks at the man who has written, in his long looping script, so many words of praise and admiration, of desire. His hair is short, dark, combed back from his face. It's hard to see his eyes clearly in both photographs, because the light is so bright he's squinting, but he has a generous face, full lips that are just about to curve into a smile, and he seems humble, and polite, the way he leans against the car, the way he folds his arms.

He doesn't know her, and yet after seeing one picture of her he offers her this.

So she writes to Phil. She includes more snaps, a cascade of questions and words that she knows will make his hands tremble. Not quite yes. Not yet. She feels her own power.

She waits, agitated, for mail every day. She lives and eats and breathes and sleeps images of pastel-coloured paper and a now easily decipherable scrawl.

✡

September 17, 1937

My dearest Bert,

I was really bucked this morning when I received your letter.

I was looking forward to one from you since I wrote to you last. I think this is my third or fourth letter to you.

As regards the snaps you enclosed, well all I can really say is that I am very much bucked with them.

I will treasure and cherish them for all times as snaps from one whom I really and truly love … just say yes to me Bert and I will do the rest …

Bertha whispers to herself as she reads over his words, *Please write soon and say 'yes', your loving (if I might say so) Phil.*

The postcards of Johannesburg show a gleaming city with modern glass buildings and wide sidewalks. People look rich. She wonders what it might be like to live south of the equator, where long obliterating winters never reach; where she is wanted; where one word from her would make a man the happiest person in the world.

Intoxicated by a draught of wild thoughts, she falls back onto her bed and closes her eyes.

She imagines that sun-drenched land. Birds sing songs she has never heard before. A man she has never met adores her day and night. Children laugh in the afternoon breeze. There is a small house, not unlike the one in Indiana, but this one is bright and open. She contrasts this picture with another one where snow falls every winter, where the mercury drops below freezing in October and in May there is still frost on the ground. Poverty is something you wear like an old coat, desperate to shake off its trappings. She tries to imagine the trees in a country beneath the equator, or the way people dress there. She pictures a family. Children. Grandchildren. Great-grandchildren. Love. Her heart aches. Perhaps the only way to truly heal from immeasurable mother-loss is as simple as a single word: yes.

She feels the tide turning towards an unknown future. Meyer knows about Phil's offer. Gerty knows now too. Bertha's heart beats hope through her veins, but she keeps her excitement hidden. She remembers a past in an orphan home, a dead mother and a distant father who makes music and no money. She remembers the cramped and freezing nights spent in a baby's crib, her eighteen-year-old skeleton folded into a foetal S-shape beneath a bathrobe. To not at least consider a life in Africa would be a kind of blindness.

In her next letter to Phil, Bertha confirms her interest in going to South Africa. She accepts Phil's kind offer. Meyer will consider his future, and the role South Africa has to play in it, in due course. In the meantime, her answer to Phil's question is indeed yes.

Bertha sits with Meyer under a maple in the last days of the Midwestern summer. Some of the leaves are already touched with gold. Fall always creeps up on them before they know it, but she will not mind this imminent autumn. Her sights are already set halfway around the world.

Meyer looks at her. Her smile is mysterious, confident. She's the Mona Lisa. She looks back at her brother, feels the pulse of the world and the magnetic pull of a far-off land. She's become an adult.

–*I wrote to Phil, Meyer.*

–*You always write to Phil.*

–*I told him yes.*

Silence. The rustling of a breath of wind through high leaves.

–*I guess I don't know how I feel about that*, Meyer says.

–*I know. But he wants you to come over too. He will do anything for me, Meyer, for us. Uncle Woolf could give you a job in one of the stores. There's nothing to lose. What do I have here? Who's here for me, besides you? He's a very decent, kind-hearted man and both Uncle Woolf and Aunt Dora think the world of him.* Bertha pauses. *I wish our mother were alive.*

–*Yep. I do too. Bert, you're the most beautiful girl in the world, and the best sister anyone could ever have. I don't know how I can let you go.*

✡

October 1937 marks the beginning of the takeover of Jewish property in Europe. President Roosevelt tries to tell the world that it is on the brink of an international disaster. His words slide over a group of young people, on the threshold of their new adult lives, as they head out into the velvet night. Bertha plans to spend her twenty-first birthday dancing with Gert, Meyer, Arleen and a troop of old home kids. Some are already married. Others have joined the army.

On her way out of the apartment that evening, she hears the president on the wireless and stops in her tracks. *The peace, the freedom, and the security of 90 per cent of the population is being jeopardised by the remaining 10 per cent, who are threatening a breakdown of all international order and law.* She closes her eyes and shuts out a seeping horror. It cannot happen again. Surely the pogroms Jacob escaped are locked in the past. The world has since come to its senses and Jewish persecution is forever behind the iron doors of history.

So then, why, just days ago, has Hitler taken over an institution for handicapped children in Württemberg, and turned it into some kind of 'Euthanasia Centre'?

It doesn't bear thinking about. She rushes into the night to celebrate her coming of age.

That night, Bertha is, in no uncertain terms, the life and soul of the party. Young men seem to appear from the ether. She is as unattainable as the sun. All they can do is stand in her light, dazzled by her radiance. Her heart belongs to a man in another hemisphere who has taken all of her love for himself.

November arrives. Ohio has been in the grip of a cold spell. All the puddles have turned to ice. The temperature in Cleveland hasn't risen above freezing for over a month. The blaze of fall colours has vanished, and the city has turned into a black-and-white version of the preceding Indian summer, which lasted into September.

It's the fifth of the month. On this day, on the other side of the world, Hitler's secret conference happens. He relays to his High

Command detailed plans to dominate Europe. The speech is recorded for future generations to look back on in horror.

It's also the day that Meyer shows Bertha a letter that he has written to Phil. When she reads it, she feels a stab of anguish for the small sibling whom she wanted to mother, and who has ended up being her guardian.

November 5, 1937

Cleveland, Ohio
U.S.A.

Dear Philip:

I'm quite sure that you will be rather surprised to receive this letter from me, but I feel that since you no doubt will be my brother-in-law, we really ought to become better acquainted.

I am under the impression that you think the only thing that is keeping Bertha from going to South Africa is me. You must understand that Bertha and I have always lived together and have become very attached to one another. Upon receipt of your first letter, I naturally would not be in favor of her going to such a far-off country. But since that first letter I have done quite a bit of thinking about the entire matter and have slowly changed my opinion of the trip. I feel that you will be happy and will make Bertha a very happy girl. I suppose I need not mention it, but I wish that you take very good care of Bertha.

As her brother I ought to be qualified to tell you a few things about her. She is a very beautiful girl, has an attractive smile, agreeable, and always aiming to please. In my estimation she would make an ideal wife. At the present she is shopping around for the trip and is trying to make both ends meet.

About myself there isn't much to say except that I am temporarily working in a jewelry store in order to save money with which to enter college next fall. I am planning to study business administration. It is a four-year course but I know that somehow I will be able to manage my money worries. I want to thank both you and my uncle for your generous offer and can't express myself in words as to how much I appreciate what you are contemplating doing for me. We'll go into further detail about everything after Bertha is settled in your country.

I neglected to mention that due to you, my cousins' letters and the actual realization of Bertha going to live in Africa makes it no longer seem like a far-away land. In fact I have already begun thinking about making a visit after I have finished college. Before closing I want to wish both you and Bertha all the luck in the world and that your marriage will be a happy and successful one.

Sincerely, Meyer

✡

It is as if the future is already written.

When the next letter from Phil arrives she opens it with trembling hands. Every romantic dream, every idealistic thought, every ounce of joy has rushed together and created a picture of a life that she is impatient to step into.

Transvaal
S. Africa

8.11.37

My darling Bert.

Happy is the man who receives good news.

Very many thanks for your lovely letter. Gee, Bert darling, you have made me a very happy man.

I can't wait for the day when I will see you land in S. Africa. I hope it won't take too long a time now.

I cabled you 97 dollars just for a few necessities and then cabled you asking you when you can leave America so that I can get your ticket for you.

All I want you to do, darling, is to get your passport in order. If they ask any questions, notify the authorities that you are coming over with the intention of getting married.

I have made all enquiries here as regards your coming over.

If you come over to get married, then you must do so within 6 months of your landing.

After you are married you make application for a South African national and everything is in order.

That is what we intend doing, isn't it, darling?

I have already spoken to Uncle Woolf and Aunt Dora. They both agree with me. In fact I believe they both wrote to you.

I don't know what Uncle Woolf wrote, because he wrote in Jewish, a language which I can't read. Aunt Dora refused to let me see her letter so that you might know more about it than I do …

That is about all there is to write, darling. My kindest regards to your brother.

Tons of love to you

Yours forever,
Phil

Yes, of course she intends to marry him. She has given him her word.

Middelburg, Transvaal, South Africa. Even the names are expansive. Bertha carefully folds the letter and Phil's love into the palm of her hand. She vows she will keep his writings forever. She will guard them always, so that one day her children and grandchildren and great-grandchildren will be able to look back into the past and see the map of this journey, which will also be theirs. She tries to envision Phil's South Africa. There is space and few people and open plains. Somewhere there are lions, perhaps even snakes, but Phil hasn't mentioned wildlife. There is plenty of money, no shortage of food, and, he promises, civilisation. It is nothing like the depressing images of freezing Cleveland. And that, for her, is enough.

✡

In Phil's letters, there is no hint of what lies ahead for his country. In 1937, when he invites Bertha to live with him in the sunshine, South Africa is recovering fast from the Great Depression. Johannesburg sits on billions of dollars' worth of gold, and African labour is dirt cheap. White South Africans are soon to have one of the highest standards of living in the world.

Ten years from this date, however, the National Party of South Africa will engineer a system of racial segregation known as apartheid. It will come into effect in 1948; under it, all black South Africans will be stripped of their nationality and millions of them will be made foreigners in their own country. They will be relegated to Bantu homelands and have to carry passbooks with them when in white areas. There will be the Prohibition of Mixed Marriages Act, the Population Registration Act, the Immorality Act, and the Group Areas Act – all of which will institutionalise racism and legalise the persecution of the majority of the population. Black people will be third-class citizens, even though they will be about 19 million strong against the 3.5 million whites. The country will be fitfully holding down revolutionary outrage, which is just waiting to destabilise privileged white society.

Because of a letter from an orphan girl to her Uncle Woolf in South Africa that changes the direction of the rushing river of time, I am born on volatile soil in a country of red earth below the Tropic of Capricorn.

✡

From November 1937, preparations are underway for Bertha's eventual passage to South Africa. She will travel aboard the SS *Berengaria.* She will depart from New York and travel to Southampton in England. From there, the *Dunbar Castle*, a less grand ship, will take her down the west coast of Africa before arriving in Cape Town.

As Bertha prepares to leave, she wonders if she will ever see her father again. She does not know that it will be fifty years before she sets foot once more on American soil.

*–Bert, you can't be serious?*

*–I leave for Africa in February. We're to be married in June.*

*–What does Meyer think of it?*

*–I guess he's all right. First he didn't think much of the idea but he's come round to it.*

*–But I can't imagine you leaving, Bert. I just saw us always being together – you marrying some nice Jewish doctor, me marrying Al or someone like him … us going to the pictures together, dancing, baking, shopping, living down the road, raising families within miles of each other …*

Gertrude's rising anguish is at odds with Bertha's expanding inner universe. She can't be swayed. Her heart is already halfway across the Atlantic.

*–Phil's a gentleman, Gert. He's going to take care of me. Uncle Woolf is the only relative who has wanted to take me and Meyer under his wing, and he'll be there for me when I arrive. Imagine that. An uncle who cares enough to help pay my passage and tell me I've got a home there forever. And maybe you can come and visit. In time.*

*–Yeah. Maybe.* Gertrude speaks without conviction. She's crying. The sky is the colour of steel and the two young women walk back to the apartment carrying bags of shopping after the day's work. It's Friday. Shabbos. Bertha's face glows. She's wearing a new hat. For the first time in her life, she doesn't mind the cold.

*–You look swell, Bert. Just grand. You could have anyone you wanted.*

*–You flatter me too much. Anyway, my heart belongs to Phil Davidow. And always will.*

*–Arleen is coming over this evening. I baked challah yesterday and we can be together like old times.*

*–That's grand, Gerty. Now, buck up and smile. Being glum doesn't suit you at all!*

✡

Jacob receives Bertha's news from Meyer. Walking along the banks of Lake Michigan, Jacob buries his hands deep in his pockets. Africa. He doesn't even know where it is. He is happy for her. Life has found his daughter and will take her towards success. Meyer has, thank goodness, his job in the jewellery store. He's saving money. He wants to be a businessman.

The clouds are low and threatening snow. What is beginning to happen in Europe chills Jacob's heart. This human race is bent on its own destruction. He fails to understand hatred or malice. His soul is the colour of winter, having experienced only three real summers: his early childhood, before the world became a terrifying place; the brief time with Ethel before the children; and the first few years with Bertha and Meyer. The single escape from his life now is in the music he plays. Even when he teaches his young students, the rich mahogany tones of the violin are Jacob's solace. When he transports others into that warmth, he knows he is doing the only meaningful thing God has allowed him. He wishes for Bertha to go to this faraway Africa and flourish.

✡

To be born in Africa at the end of the 1960s means to be moulded by the forces of a raw and turbulent continent. To learn to walk on that gold-rich earth means to feel shuddering quakes when the mines collapse. To be held in the warm black arms of a comforting nanny means to take in the heartache of oppressed millions, and to feel the black woman's heart divide – because while she wants to love you, you are white, and her own children have to live six months away from her in one of the Bantu homelands. She sees them twice a year. Her only reason for holding you is so she can feed her own family.

To arrive in South Africa as a new, white immigrant in the 1930s will mean to acquire immediate superior social status to the 19 million black people who live there; it will mean to dare to imagine a future in which the weight of the past evaporates in subtropical sunlight.

✡

Beyond the flurry of activity and shopping, the snow buries the sidewalk outside the apartment in Ohio. Bertha visits Bellefaire and tells Jack Girick and Michael Sharlitt her news. Her happiness is uncontainable, infectious.

Then, reporters from *The Cleveland Herald*, *The New York Times* and *Universal News* get wind of her story: an orphan girl is preparing to leave on a life-changing journey to Africa, to marry a man she has never met. Bertha grants an exclusive interview to the Cleveland paper, and takes delight in turning the others down. The article comes out with separate photographs of her and Phil, under the heading: *They'll Wed in Africa.*

Michael Sharlitt puts her in touch with good friends in New York, the kindly Dr and Mrs Mintz, who promise to take care of Bertha and see her safely onto the SS *Berengaria*. Bertha establishes other points of familiarity on her journey: one of the home girls, Rose Rosker, is also living in New York City and promises to see her off as well. She's not Bertha's closest friend, but she's a lovely girl and the thought of her being there is reassuring. Along the way, she trusts there will be small lights illuminating her passage to a new world.

All these details begin to make the journey inescapably real. Phil sends more money so that Bertha can purchase all she needs. She's never been taken care of like this before. She has never spent a single cent that she hasn't earned, until now. And boy, does it feel grand, she thinks.

–*You know, Arleen, I feel like a film star*, she says, bustling out of the May Company Department Store and wrapping a scarf around her neck too many times.

–*I say, Bert, you could be a film star. That Phil is one lucky man.*

–*Yep. And I'm one lucky gal!*

*–It will be so sad to see you go. But I wish that all your dreams come true and that you become the person you're meant to be, Bert.*

*–Thanks, Arleen. You'll write me every week, won't you?*

*–You bet.*

One of the last things Bertha has to do is hand in her resignation at the store.

*–I'm most disappointed*, Mr Goldberg says. *You are one of the store's most reliable, friendly and engaging employees. Bertha, with us you could have gone far.*

*–Thank you for the compliment, Mr Goldberg*, she says, as she tosses her hair back from her face. She walks out into the cold and breathes in the sharp, clear air. Goodbye, Cleveland.

As a farewell gift, Meyer gives Bertha a journal.

*–Write everything down*, he says. *That way, it will never be forgotten. Even the little things.*

Bertha promises she will. From the very beginning, she writes as though she's aware of an invisible future gaze, diligently bearing witness. For those who read her words in the next century, she emerges as an eternal 21-year-old with a heart full of dreams.

Saying goodbye to her beloved brother is unbearable. The only comfort is his promise that once she is settled in South Africa, he will finish his business course and join her. But World War II is a dark cloud rolling in on the horizon. It will interrupt their plans: Meyer will find himself drafted into the army and living in France. More than a decade will pass before the siblings are reunited.

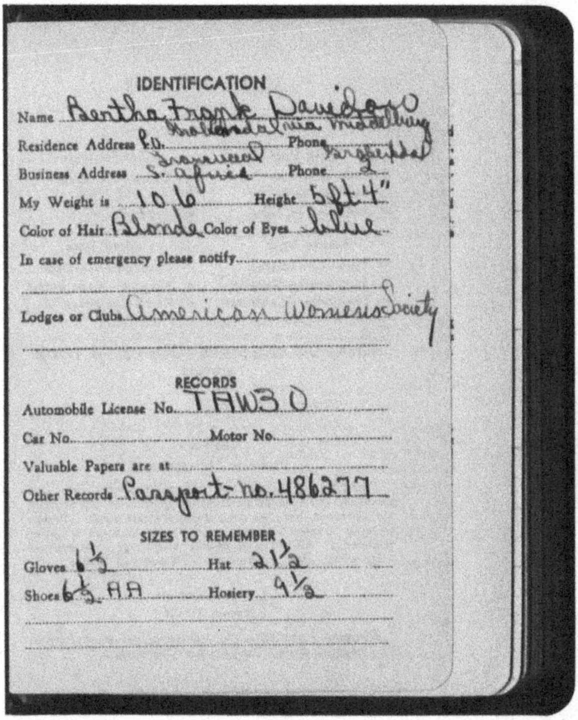

IDENTIFICATION

Name Bertha Frank Davidow

Residence Address P.O. ... Phone

Business Address S. Africa ... Phone

My Weight is 106 Height 5ft 4"

Color of Hair Blonde Color of Eyes blue

In case of emergency please notify

Lodges or Clubs American Women's Society

RECORDS

Automobile License No. TAW3 0

Car No. Motor No.

Valuable Papers are at

Other Records Passport no. 486277

SIZES TO REMEMBER

Gloves 6½ Hat 21½

Shoes 6½ AA Hosiery 9½

# PART TWO

*1938 January 22, resigned my job from May Co. Spent a few days in Chicago Ill. Left for New York January 31.*

*Doctor and Mrs. Mintz drove me all over New York City. Was amazed about the structure of buildings, skyscrapers – saw City Hall.*

New York, 1938: Bertha feels on top of the world. The buildings seem to be there for her benefit alone, to tell her that life is waiting for her. This is the gateway to the world, she thinks, looking across the water at the Statue of Liberty. The future in all its enormity and promise is written in every sign in Times Square, in the vastness of City Hall, and in the fashions of the very rich as they walk down Park Avenue.

At midnight on the eve of her departure, the temperature falls well below freezing. She wakes up in the darkness and thinks: *1938 – the year that will usher me into a new world.*

The *SS Berengaria* is one of the world's largest ocean liners at the time. It's 919 feet long and 99 feet wide. Tourist class is quite luxurious. The beds are wide, while comfortable chairs and a table create the impression of a hotel suite. Bertha sits on her berth, elated. *Africa*, she thinks, *here I come!*

Games of shuffleboard, nightly films and dancing fill in the time which becomes distance: the space between Meyer and her, between home and the *Berengaria*, increases with every hour.

The deep green Atlantic carries her ship across the waves. Years before, another young immigrant, Jacob David Frank, travelled across these waters towards his new life. His heart did not know what life would offer him, what legacy he would leave in the ephemeral parts of his soul. With each passing minute, Bertha retraces Jacob's journey backwards. She could never have imagined that twenty-five years after he crossed the Atlantic to escape the horrors of persecution, she would cross it again.

Bertha has left behind everyone she knows and loves. Although the word 'courage' wouldn't immediately spring to her mind, it is not hard to see that the fabric of her soul is woven out of this fine substance.

*February 5*
*Feel terribly blue tonite – miss everyone so much.*

After a week aboard the ship, Bertha meets three charming young men: Mr Donald Patrick, a most charming aviator from New York; Mr Mack Heller, an attentive Jewish boy; and Mr Gainor Jackson, a New Zealander who has been visiting his sister in America. The four of them are sitting together. Gainor Jackson has mastered several card tricks, which are the source of excitement and laughter at the table.

*–That's impossible!* Bertha exclaims as he picks her chosen card from the deck. *How do you do that?*

*–I told you. Magic. I can read your mind.* He winks at her. Bertha can feel her cheeks flaming. She laughs at Gainor's jokes but is

conscious of not flirting. She must not encourage any of them, she thinks, observing how easily they could misinterpret her appreciation of their humour.

Over the next week, the three men compete for her attention as though she is the only woman on board: it's a case of which creature might move in closest to the source of heat and light. Her beauty is inadvertent. Its substance is partly generated by the heartbreak and euphoria of someone on the knife-edge between desperate hope and the compelling weight of a tragic curve. Bertha tries to engage equally with each of her admirers, though she is particularly drawn to one of them.

The night wraps blue arms around the rocking ship. Two people are standing on the deck. The sun has already blazed into the sea. The wind has tangled Bertha's hair into a whirl in front of her face. Mr Jackson, she now knows, is twenty-seven. He must be well over six foot tall; when he smiles, the moonlight falls on dimples in his cheeks, and his right eyebrow is raised almost permanently in ironic surprise. Bertha feels his gaze on her. *Be careful, girl*, she tells herself. It's okay for *him* to be smitten, but her heart is sealed and her feelings won't be allowed out, even though her pulse races with anticipation.

*–Bertha, will you marry me?*

*–What?* She bursts out laughing and puts her hand over her mouth, her eyes meeting his. *Mr Jackson, you can't be serious!* Her eyes sparkle. She desperately wants to play down this interaction as no more than light-hearted banter.

*–Well, I know you're engaged to a man you've never met, but I can't help but give this a go. Will you consider marrying me, Miss Bertha Frank?*

She's doing her best to hold her emotions in check. She prays for strength. As the present collides with her future, she knows she must keep her focus on the journey ahead.

*–Mr Jackson, you know that's impossible. But I promise you, we'll be friends. When you get to New Zealand I promise to write you, and hope that you'll write back.*

He takes a deep, uneven breath and turns to the waves. *It's a deal, my dear. Friends we shall be.*

His dimples have disappeared, but a moment later they reappear and he says: *Shall we go in? It's getting really cold out here.*

He will keep his promise. Every year until his death, he will send her a postcard at Christmas time.

*February 8*
*The sight of land this morning gave me a start. Strange to see Europe. The first port we docked was Cherbourg, France. I never dreamed I would ever be going abroad to the other side of the world …*

Beneath its beautiful green exterior, the continent is simmering. The first of ten thousand Jewish children are huddling, waiting to be transported to England in anticipation of something sinister. The young woman aboard the SS *Berengaria* doesn't feel it. She is amazed at people's accents as they board the ship.

The *Berengaria* makes its steady way towards Southampton. Bertha stands on deck with Mr Jackson, the wind blowing their hair back. She contemplates a million possible futures.

London is a lifetime away from America already. Buildings are not nearly as tall as they are in New York. Streets are narrow and people speak quietly. Their accents remind Bertha of radio broadcasters reading the news.

She spends the day with Gainor Jackson by her side, unimposing, present. He tells her stories of Shakespeare and soldiers, of the love-sick poet Keats, who longed for immortality with such desperation that he wrote himself into eternity. They drink strong aromatic tea from India in porcelain cups and they eat English scones. He buys her books and talks about the British Empire and how big it is now. Once, when the breeze tosses her hair into her eyes, he reaches over and smooths it away from her forehead.

His kindness, his willingness to step back with such grace, is radiance, and she basks in it. They laugh their way across London, watch the changing of the guard at Buckingham Palace and stand in awe beneath stained glass windows in Westminster Abbey. At the end of the day Bertha dares to imagine, in the pale February light in England, another possible future. What if he were the man she had been destined to marry? As they cover the wet London streets, she is in danger of falling for him.

She redirects all her thoughts to where they need to be: with the man who has opened his soul to her and whose heart is bringing her across the world.

*February 11*
*... Mr Jackson escorted me to the train and saw that I was alright. The scenery was lovely, green grass of fields. Homes built close together. So I bid London goodbye for my next voyage to S. Africa where I hope and pray my future will hold happiness, health and a beloved husband-to-be Philip Davidow waiting for me ...*

✡

After the *Berengaria*, and after the excitement of palaces and abbeys, the *Dunbar Castle* is a real downer. The berths are narrow, the decor faded and scrappy. The service is shocking. Instead of Americans, British passengers fill the dining room and the decks, and for all her efforts to be cheerful and engaging, she comes up against a wall of cool disregard wherever she turns. The message, although unspoken, is clear: *Keep to yourself.*

The bottom has fallen out of the world, and now the centre too. She is restless. A grey sadness descends. She wills her thoughts away from Gainor Jackson and writes seventy postcards to people back home, giving herself dimension, location. The words she sends are written by a brave explorer of foreign lands.

Now, more than ever, she longs for her mother.

After a few days of joyless time-wasting on board, Bertha's attention is drawn to a young man. He seems to be wherever she is, and finally comes over to her on deck to make her acquaintance.

–*May I have the pleasure?* he says. *I'm Harold Feldman, originally from London, travelling to South Africa, God help us all, and hoping to begin a new life there.*

–*I'm Bertha Frank from Cleveland, Ohio. Pleased to meet you*, she says and holds out her good hand.

–*Only pleased? Don't I stand out at all from this rabble? Well, you certainly do, and it's a delight to meet you, Bertha. Fancy a drink?*

Harold is smart and irreverent. His easy-going manner and dry humour are infectious. She is in need of companionship, and immediately warms to him.

–*Where are you going?* she asks him.

–*Johannesburg*, he says. *The city of gold. I'm already ecstatic at the thought of leaving miserable, God-forsaken England forever. And the talk of war is enough to make anyone quite sick. What about you, Miss Frank from Cleveland, Ohio?*

–*I'm going to South Africa to marry the man who's paying my passage over.*

–*Oh well, that's a pity!*

–*What, that I'm going to South Africa?* Her eyes gleam with mischief.

*–Nope! That you're planning to marry a man who's simply paying your passage. I'll pay your passage!*

She laughs. *Too late.*

*–Well, if you don't like your husband-to-be, I'll offer to wait as a replacement.*

Bertha laughs again and looks away at the night sky. She has never seen stars like this. They go all the way down to the far horizon. They are so bright they look almost within reach.

*–Jokes aside, Bertha. That's rather a brave thing to do.*

*–Yep, I guess so.*

*February 15*

*... We are heading for the South now towards the equator. The sunset on the sea is gloriously colourful. Turquoise skies, orange pale pink blue and beautiful sun rays sprouting like fireworks into the heavens. At night the sea is midnight black ... the heavens at night are sprinkled with the everlasting shimmering stars ...*

Now that Harold has moved himself out of the backdrop of cardboard people, others dare to do so too. Donald McGee is from Scotland and has flaming red hair. She can tell from the outset that the same fire runs through his veins. He is witty and easily upset. The situation mirrors the one aboard the *Berengaria*. Bertha is accustomed to allowing the delicate threads of friendship and warmth to weave between her and her male shipmates, even as they compete for her attention and do their best to win her over. The end they each want is futile, but that seems to matter little in the present moment.

The *Dunbar Castle* comes into port in Gran Canaria, the most inhabited of all the Canary Islands. The Spanish archipelago lies 838 miles from Europe, and just over 50 miles from the edge of the African continent.

Bertha is overwhelmed by all the colour. The houses are brightly painted. The people are dark and striking. This is her first true encounter with a new culture. Donald McGee escorts her through Las Palmas and keeps her arm in his. Protection, he says, against the handsome señors who would no doubt spirit her away given even the smallest chance. For the first time, she encounters children poorer than any she has seen, who run up to the visiting Europeans and beg for a few coins, or even for cigarettes.

–*We're lucky in America*, she says to Don. *This level of poverty is appalling.*

–*Welcome to the real world, m'dear.*

Through the streets they dodge donkey carts and poorly maintained streetcars. Some of the local housing is all stone, with few windows. She learns that the climate is warm all year round, and the lack of windows keeps the heat out in summer.

At the end of the day, when the passengers once again board the *Dunbar Castle*, Harold Feldman comes to meet Bertha. He gives Donald a cursory glance and says with a twinkle in his eye, *I've been looking for you all day. Will you join me for dinner?*

–*Yep. I'll see you at seven.*

She thanks Don for a wonderful day and excuses herself to go to her cabin. He suddenly storms away without saying a word, leaving her blinking in his angry slipstream.

*February 17*

*... Don McGee is angry at me and he acts like a child ... Feel very moody tonight.*

The equator beckons, and as the ship carries its passengers further south, colours everywhere intensify. Never has the sky been this blue, nor clouds this blinding. The deep Atlantic Ocean is turquoise and the white-tipped waves support the hull of the boat, rocking it slightly from side to side. Bertha is intoxicated by the sun. Its warmth is everywhere and saturates her until she feels quite drunk.

Donald apologises on deck for being a grump.

Deck tennis becomes Bertha's new forte. She relishes her new-found talent. Her back is peeling after the worst sunburn of her life, but she breathes through the pain and welcomes the kiss of the tropics, more than pleased that she will arrive in South Africa bathed already in the glow of equatorial rays.

*February 18*
*The sun is very hot. My legs prickling … burned by the tropical sun. It's so good to see sunshine all around you. The ocean caps are playing leap-frog. White shines over the wide sea, blue green … have fortunately but unexpectedly won the game of deck tennis – my first attempt at playing the game.*

*February 19*
*Played doubles deck tennis. Won by serving points. Took sun bath and I'm badly burnt. Donald and I are very good friends …*

*February 20*
*Have been sailing now close to three weeks on my long journey to Africa. The sea is a lovely deep green color and the sky blue and the white clouds make beautiful pictures to the imagination but it's real.*

*February 21*
*Sat on deck, fell asleep wondering what the new world holds in store for me.*

Bertha is gathering her things together after a sleepy afternoon on the sun-drenched deck, when Harold Feldman's shadow blocks out her light.

–*You are seriously trying to cook yourself, my dear*, he says. His smile hints at nervousness. Or perhaps she's just dizzy with heat. *May I sit?*

–*Sure. If you can move my stuff out of the way.*

He places himself down at the foot-end of the long wooden deck chair.

–*Bertha, I have a serious question, and I do hope you will consider it.*

–*Well, then, you'd better ask, hadn't you?* Hardly are the words out of her mouth than she realises that his question is of the serious kind, and that her playful tone doesn't match the look on his face.

–*You remember what I said about being a replacement husband if things didn't work out between you and Phil Davidow?*

–*I guess I do.*

–*Well, I was only half-joking, and I didn't even know you yet. Now that I've had the pleasure of your good company for these past eight days, I have to say I've grown very fond of you. Extraordinarily fond. Now I know that you say you already have a commitment in Africa, but since nothing's signed, and you haven't even met the fellow, here's my first question: do you like me?*

–*I'm sure I do, Harold, but …*

–*All right. Now, moving along, would you consider marrying me, Bertha? I shall be forever in your service as a most faithful and deserving husband.*

Deja vu. She looks into Harold's pleading eyes and knows what she must say.

–*Harold, you're a kind man, and a good shipmate. But I can't marry you, or anyone else. I'm going to marry Phil Davidow in South Africa. I've given him my word, and I will keep to that. You're a good friend, and I would sure like it if you'd be a guest at our wedding. I do like you.*

The light is fading. Venus rises like a flare over the Atlantic. Its reflection breaks and shatters in the waves and Harold looks at his shiny shoes. The equator lies behind them.

*–Let's pledge tonight, Bertha. You and I. Shipmates forever.*

*–Shipmates forever.*

The narrative flow of her life is beginning to follow a recognisable theme. She will arrive in Cape Town with two marriage proposals and a handful of heartbreaks in her wake – one of them, to some degree, her own.

✡

That night, the African continent lies just to the left of the *Dunbar Castle*. The young woman whose life will be lived out on its surface cannot comprehend the mercilessness of the country that will claim her. Her wardrobe is entirely based on an indoor world, on city life. She has dresses for parties, both formal and informal occasions, nightdresses, and beautiful hats and scarves; she has nothing for days of dust and malaria-carrying mosquitoes and red ticks that bury their heads deep in human flesh. She has no clothes for the banks of the

Olifants River, where the densest concentration of Nile crocodiles in southern Africa bask lazily in the sun and wait for stupid sweet-fleshed humans to stray too near. The new world waits for her, its passions and predators unknown.

In the next century, when Bertha's granddaughter is twenty-two (Bertha's age at the time she leaves Ohio), she will pack her bags for the Midwest in America, her heart full of dreams. She will follow her grandmother's footsteps in reverse and, with her new husband, chase the American dream. I am that girl who leaves the place of her birth with Africa's pulse in her veins and a suitcase full of the wrong clothes. When I embark on this journey, I will have no idea about the absence of light and colour, about how to live through the freezing North American winters, nor how the buildings will press down on me where I live, just north of the city of Chicago, where my great-grandfather lost his dreams. I will be driven by idealism and the desire to escape an Africa riddled with violent crime and the absence of mercy.

✡

In their last days aboard the *Dunbar Castle*, Bertha and Harold spend all their time together. They play deck tennis, and although she tires easily, she persists, competitive, determined.

–*You're fearsome*, Harold tells her. *I pity anyone who tries to come up against you.*

*March 3*
*Ship delayed. Will leave boat tomorrow. Philip walking the decks waiting to see me.*

✡

And then, finally, rising out of the deep Indian-meeting-Atlantic Ocean: the Cape of Good Hope. For a long time, violent currents around the cape ripped ships to shreds and dashed explorers to pieces against the rocks. In Camões's *The Lusiads*, the Titan Adamastor kept guard over the entrance to the southern tip of Africa. The ancient seafarers might have wondered why the mythical giant wanted to hold back these white explorers from the African continent. They wouldn't have foreseen the centuries of strife and bloodshed, the storms that would rage across the continent as cultures and ways of life collided and boiled, as the cold Benguela current met the warm Agulhas current. Perhaps the Titan was trying to protect the KhoiKhoi people, who had been living peacefully in the area for the previous 1500 years. Perhaps the Titan knew that living on such a landmass meant diving into the conflicting currents of icy despair and fiery hope.

Nonetheless, when Bertha stares up at the face of that first imposing mountain, its hidden flecks of quartz catching the sunlight, when she understands that this is hers, her heart fills to bursting with hope, and she is ready to cry with joy.

The *Dunbar Castle* finally docks in Table Bay. Table Mountain is 3500 feet above sea level. Its flat top is blanketed with cloud, which cascades down the sides of the mountain before its edges disappear into fine, invisible mist.

Bertha is shaking as she makes her way down the gangplank and onto the solid ground of the harbour wharf. Anticipation makes her weak. She thinks: *What if we don't click?*

And then she is being lifted off her feet by a short older man with woolly hair and kind, kind eyes, and Bertha hugs him back for all she's worth.

–*Uncle Woolf!* she exclaims. And then, *Phil!*

–*At last*, Phil says and smiles. *You made it.*

He's standing nervously behind Uncle Woolf, but as soon as her uncle lets her go, he steps towards her and hugs her to himself, and his arms tell her she is here, she is home, and he will love her for the rest of his life.

His body shakes in her embrace, but his smile is generous. His deep brown eyes speak of devotion and sacrifice. She knows this sense of warmth: it's trust. *Yep*, she thinks, catching his eye, *this could work out.*

–*You're even more beautiful than I ever imagined*, Phil says. *Those snaps don't do the real you any justice. I can't believe you've arrived!* He takes her arm. She attempts to conceal her deformity by balling her hand into a fist, but he notices her anxiety.

–*Let's see that birth defect you were so worried about, darling Bertha.*

She slowly uncurls her fingers and feels blood rush to her face.

–*My darling Bert. I can't believe you were worried about this. To me, you are perfect.* He wraps her hand in his.

*March 4*

*At last. Africa.*

*Excited when I met Philip. He has a nice smile. Uncle Woolf is adorable. Spent the day with Phil in Cape Town. It's a lovely city. Table Mountain is spectacular … On train to Johannesburg. Feeling very blue.*

*March 5*

*On train second nite. I am actually beginning to fall in love with Philip. He is very sweet.*

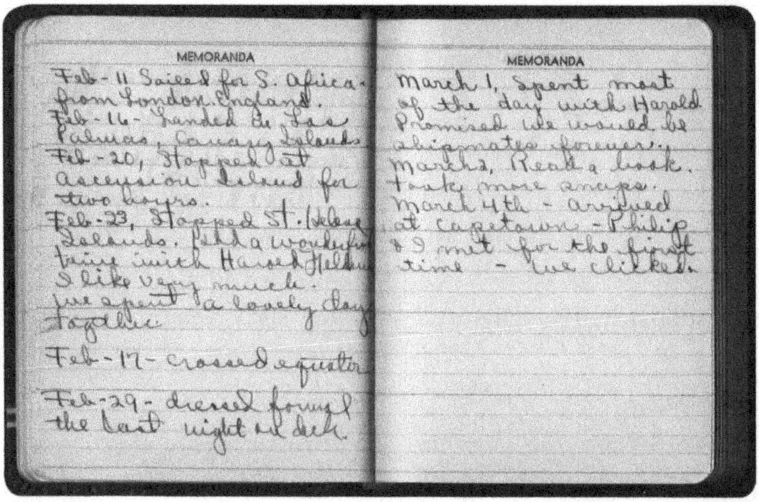

MEMORANDA

Feb-11 Sailed for S. Africa from London, England.
Feb-16- Landed in Las Palmas, Canary Islands.
Feb-20, Stopped at Ascension Island for two hours.
Feb-23, Stopped St. Helena Islands. Had a wonderful time with Harold [illegible] I like very much. We spent a lovely day together
Feb-17- crossed equator
Feb-29- dressed formal the last night on deck.

MEMORANDA

March 1, Spent most of the day with Harold Promised we would be shipmates forever.
March 2, Read a book. took more snaps.
March 4th - arrived at capetown - Philip & I met for the first time - we clicked.

✡

All the way from Cape Town to Johannesburg, the train rocks them towards their destiny. Uncle Woolf is in his own compartment so that the young couple can have some time to get to know each other. Through the window, Bertha sees quaint Cape Dutch houses, with their gabled walls and whitewashed exteriors from the seventeenth century, as the train leaves the populated areas. At first the landscape is mountainous, but the further they travel north, the more sparse the landscape becomes. Eventually, evening falls and the train hits the Karoo desert. There is nothing but sand and scrub as far as the eye can see. It's so dry Bertha tastes the dust. Darkness descends, and she's amazed at how rapidly all the colours fade to blue, then black. There is no sign of human habitation.

Sitting in the train compartment, with the bunks folded down to make a comfortable couch, Bertha feels her heart sink.

The conductor comes in and asks for their tickets in a foreign language, and Phil speaks back to him in the same rough tongue that sounds like German to her ears.

*–Alle kaartjies asseblief. All tickets please.*

*–Hierso, meneer.*

*–Baie dankie meneer, mevrou.*

*–Goodness, Phil, what language is that?* She's stepped into another universe in which she is partially illiterate. The emptiness of the Karoo, the strange sounds of an incomprehensible tongue, her new life … suddenly, the magnitude of what she's done makes her feel ill.

*–Are you all right, darling?*

*–I'm sure I am. Just a minute. Maybe I need a glass of water.*

*–Gee, Bert, darling, you gave me a fright. Your face went so pale for a moment. It's time for dinner anyway. Give me your hand, my beautiful Bert. Let me treat you to more than a glass of water.*

His very being is kindness. He is gallant, caring, devoted. In his eyes she sees the shimmer of disbelief – how impossibly true it is that she has arrived. He saw a snap and fell in love with her image. He had the courage to ask. She had the courage to come. All the way from Ohio to South Africa. He holds her hand as though she is made of the most precious substance in the galaxy. If she did not already love the man who wrote her such letters, she loves him now.

✡

Johannesburg, city of gold, iGoli. The train arrives in the glittering morning. The air is fresh and the bride- and groom-to-be step onto the station platform with Uncle Woolf. Guiding Bertha as if he has been by her side all her life, he hastens her towards a woman who tries to embrace them all in her ample arms.

*–May I introduce you to my darling wife, Dora. Phil's sister and your dear aunt.*

*–Aunt Dora! Pleased to meet you.*

*–Isn't she grand?* Phil grins, wrapping his arm around his future wife.

*–Welcome to South Africa, Bertha my dear. We have a lunch prepared for you, and your cousins can't wait to meet you. I hope all this won't be too overwhelming … oh, and our old mother is beside herself with excitement and can hardly wait for a visit from you. Come on, Woolf, hurry up – will you go and get the baggage with Phil, we haven't got all day!* Her accent, like Phil's, is sort of English. There's a slight edge of something foreign – it's as if she might be German, or Dutch.

Bertha is heartened by what she sees. Johannesburg is a modern city. It looks like parts of Cleveland, but the buildings are more square, and lower, and the sun is so bright as to be blinding. Motorcars line the streets and smartly dressed men and women hurry down the sidewalks.

And then she sees black people. More black people than she has ever set eyes on in her life. They are so dark as to be almost indigo. And yet, though she has no idea, their being in the city at all is tightly regulated by a system called influx control. The architects of what will soon become known as apartheid are already hard at work. Only a certain number of African people can live in slums like Orlando just outside the city centre. The rest of them have to reside in 'homelands', designated areas far from the city, which makes it almost impossible to find work. When World War II begins, the law will be temporarily amended to allow for cheap mining labour as all the young white men are conscripted.

Phil notes her wide eyes and gestures to the black people who walk on the opposite side of the street, keeping a polite and fearful distance from the legal white citizens of the country and anyone else with light skin.

*–Our kaffirs are good people. They're respectful, helpful and decent most of the time. They know their place. You'll see many more of them once we get to Middelburg. And you'll get used to them soon enough.*

In 1938, 'kaffir' is still an everyday term. No one in the small party walking from the station in Johannesburg is aware of how potent that word will be in just a few decades. By the 1970s, calling anyone a 'kaffir' will be an actionable offence. The word will be deemed the most derogatory one possible. Its origins lie hundreds of years in the past: 'kaffir' was the Arabic word meaning 'unbeliever', referring to every non-Muslim, or anyone who hid themselves from the bright light of Islam. The word's meaning was mistaken by early colonials in North Africa who thought it referred to indigenous people. And so the term travelled all the way down the continent.

*–Most of them are good people. But you've got to keep alert and watch them*, Uncle Woolf says. *There are many more of them than us.*

With Phil's protective arm around her, they load the luggage into a waiting car. A tall, dark-haired man in a suit opens the door and doffs his hat.

*–Good morning*, he says. *I'm Joshua Lourie. Welcome to South Africa. Now can we get going, please? It's like waiting for the Queen with you people.*

Bertha looks into his piercing, humourless eyes and her smile falters. He is, in that moment, the most uncompromising presence she's ever encountered. Perhaps she's just tired, but he seems terrifying. His large hands assist Bertha into the car, where she crushes herself into Phil's warm arm. Phil whispers in her ear over the loud automobile engine, *He's the fiance of your cousin Mildred Braker, my niece. Don't be bothered by him. He's not that much of a patient or tolerant person.*

*No*, Bertha thinks, staring at the back of his neck and thick hair, *he's more than that. He's downright rude.*

And then Bertha finds herself in a suburb of Johannesburg, in a beautiful house belonging to Phil's older sister, and in the middle of a large family with all her closest blood relatives, who ironically are Phil's too. It's overwhelming. She's treated like royalty. Her cousins, Phil's nieces, instantly adore her and wish to show her everything and ask her everything, and more than anything they express how much they want her to be happy and to love South Africa. Uncle Woolf has taken her under his wing and treats her with the same affection as he treats his own daughters. She could not be happier.

Over lunch and dinner, Bertha shines. Her cousins hang on her every word, devouring her American accent. She bathes and changes and the girls, who she has decided are quite charming, admire and envy her fashionable American clothes. Phil falls more deeply in love with every passing moment and professes his adoration almost as frequently.

The only dark cloud in the room is the presence of Joshua, cousin Mildred's fiance. He skulks in the corners and smokes on the verandah. He paces restlessly about, disdainful of the small talk and petty concerns of the chattering women.

At teatime, Bertha decides that if she doesn't make a friend out of him soon, she will surely go away hating him, and that could prove disastrous if they are to be family for the rest of their lives.

She whispers in Mildred's ear:

*–I'm going to have a word with your fiance. We didn't get off to a grand start. What does he like to talk about?*

Her cousin shrugs. *Business, always business. Don't take it personally if he's rude, though.* She seems resigned to her fate. Resigned to a life with someone who seems to have no sense of good behaviour at all. Bertha finds the thought quite disgusting. She feels grateful for Phil.

Bertha saunters out to where Joshua stands on the verandah. She leans against a solid red brick pillar and the sun drenches half of her in yellow light. Her hair is wild and flecked with gold. She is at the height of her beauty, at the height of her power. At this moment, she feels it. Red and pink roses are blooming on a bush just in front of him. The air is full of their fragrance.

*–Apologies for making you wait earlier, Mr Lourie. I had a lot of luggage, coming from America and all.*

He turns the full force of his gaze on her. She hadn't noticed before that his eyes were ice blue. Her heart pounds for no good reason, and then she's astounded when he gives her a disarming smile.

*–I'm the one who should apologise*, he says. *I'm not a patient man.* Most ordinary human beings would look away, at the garden, at the strange birds calling from the sky, but he doesn't let up. He keeps his eyes fixed on her face. Bertha holds his gaze.

*–So, what's your line of business, Mr Lourie?*

*–For God's sake, call me Joshua, will you?*

*–It's just ... we haven't properly introduced ourselves in a polite way.*

*–And? I don't think much of social etiquette.*

*–Well, I'm sure of that!*

He smiles again, unexpectedly, and drops his cigarette on the stone verandah, grinding it out beneath his heel.

*–I like a woman who can give as good as she gets*, he says. *Say, you weren't really interested in knowing what I do for a living, were you?*

*–No. I was just making conversation. But if you'd care to tell me, I'd like to hear it now. We've successfully made it beyond that first awkward moment.*

*–I'm glad we can be honest with one another. No, I wouldn't want to bore you. I do this and that. I buy, I sell. I make money. What do you do, Bertha Frank?*

The way he says her name unsettles her. It's soft, intimate.

*–I worked for the May Company Department Store in Cleveland. Now I'm about to be married, and I hope to be a good wife.*

*–I hope you're not making a big mistake, Bertha.*

*–Well, that's not a very nice thing to say.*

*–No? But it's the truth. I do hope that. You need a strong man, not a lovesick puppy-dog.*

*–I came here to make friends with you, Mr Lourie. If you insist on being rude, I'll leave you now.*

*–Don't mistake me, Bertha. This isn't rudeness. It's honesty. You're obviously a beauty, and a clever girl, and I'd hate to see you throw yourself away on someone not worthy of everything you are.*

*–Well, excuse me! And who would you, who knows everything, it seems, imagine to be someone worthy of everything I am?* Her tone is not merely sarcastic but angry, and she's not expecting the reply he gives her.

*–Me.*

Bertha turns away from him. She acknowledges her failure: she bows her head in a curt nod and walks inside. Cousin Mildred is subdued and quiet and says glumly, *I told you so. Don't take anything he said personally. He's just like that. Rude to just about everyone.*

Bertha can scarcely look at her. She's still reeling from what he's just said.

*–Why are you marrying him, then?*

*–Because he's a good man, good at business, and he'll take care of me.*

✡

Mildred Braker is right. Her husband will take care of her and of his family. In time, he will become a rich and ruthless businessman.

✡

All the bedrooms are down a long corridor. Hers is at the end. Before bedtime, Phil knocks at the door.

*–Come in!*

*–Darling Bert,* he says. His smile is warm and as open as the expansive highveld. He sits down on the edge of her bed and takes both her hands in his. She shrinks back.

*–I told you I loved you just as you are. And I do. Believe me when I tell you: you are perfect.* He takes her left hand to his lips, and presses kisses onto her tiny fingers. Her eyes fill with tears.

*–Do you think you can love me, Bert? Do you?*

*–Of course, Phil. I do.*

*March 9*
*Philip and I spent hours together. I love him so much. It's marvelous to be loved by one so dear.*

✡

The journey from Johannesburg to Groblersdal, via Middelburg, is one in which the young passenger in the front seat of the car uses all her inner reserve to stop herself from crumbling. Open country spreads out all around the spluttering car. Automobiles, she notes, drive on the wrong side of the road. The veld, as Phil calls it, is full of wandering Africans driving their cattle. Bertha's never seen anything like this before. All the comforts of the city, the buildings and landmarks that she recognises as signs of human habitation and civilisation, have vanished.

*–You will love the bushveld,* Phil promises, perceiving her fear. *I know it must feel strange, darling, and I know what I have asked you to do by coming here, but believe you me, you will get used to being out in the country. You will be awed by its beauty. Do you know, we even have lions, cheetahs, elephants, zebras and giraffes in the near vicinity? I can't wait to show you the house, Bert, darling. I have had a room*

*made up for you. It's my room, and will eventually be our room, and I hope you will find everything to your liking. Our native servants will make you very comfortable.*

Perhaps what she feels is the weight of the future. There's joy, but it's tempered by an indeterminate sense of loss; as the emptiness ahead of the car widens ahead of them, her fears could be based on a future reality: the lack of facilities in the African bush spells loss. It will mean the difference between life and death.

✡

The first stop is at the general store, which backs onto Uncle Woolf's and Aunt Dora's home. They have chickens and a big backyard and dogs, and even sheep and goats.

Many native Africans run from the house to the car as it arrives. Two boys of about three, wearing shirts and no pants, are running after a chicken. The red soil has stained their feet and they glance up at the richly dressed foreigner who steps out of the car. They point and laugh at the feather in her hat.

Groblersdal is a one-street town with the general store, the emporium, a butcher, a fruit shop, a dry cleaner and a colonial-style hotel.

The shop is full of customers.

Next stop is Phil's house. It's a kilometre from town, and will be Bertha's home.

The house is made of red brick. Bush and sand surround it. Chickens scratch in the dirt. Beyond the house are goats and sheep and the servants' quarters. Even further than that, the whole of southern Africa rolls out in undulating hills and rocky outcrops. The bushveld is still green at this time of year; the rainy season is apparently only just coming to an end.

As they get out of the car, natives appear at the door.

*–Don't worry*, Phil tells her, *Phineas will get your luggage. These people are our house servants. This is Anna, she does the cooking and cleaning. Anna, kan jy asseblief die mevrou die kombuis wys?*

Anna curtsies but does not take the hand that Bertha extends. Both women look at one another in stunned silence. Bertha turns to her husband-to-be.

*–Is that African you're speaking, Phil?*

*–No! Well, yes, Afrikaans. Most of the kaffirs in the area speak Afrikaans, and their native languages. Anna is going to show you the kitchen, darling, and then I'll show you your bedroom. You can speak to Anna in English, she speaks a little.*

The kitchen is large. It's the size of the entire apartment in Cleveland. The floors are made of stone. Giant stainless-steel pots sit on the stove, boiling away. There is only a single tap with running water in the house. The other water source is outside, attached to a large rain tank. Beyond the kitchen is a living room, also huge by her standards. Then a dark, cool corridor and three bedrooms, one of them made up with a rose-patterned coverlet and a vase full of white arum lilies on the mahogany dresser.

Bertha gazes out at the view from her new bedroom window. Lions? Cheetahs? In the vicinity? She can't find herself, can't make sense of this. Is she the same girl from the Jewish Orphan Home in Ohio who, just weeks ago, had never travelled further than Chicago?

In the evening, the African sun descends in a blaze of colour. She and Phil are finally alone in the living room.

*–Are the natives here all the time?*

*–Do you mean our servants? Yes, every day except Sundays.*

*–You've got yourself a regular nudist colony here, Phil.*

He laughs and leans over to embrace her. *Yes, it's just their way.*

*Don't be surprised. Sometimes the native women don't cover their breasts, and the children don't wear clothes when it's warm.*

*–Are they poor, Phil?*

*–Yes, but they have enough to eat and roofs over their heads. You'll get used to it all, in time. Anna will help in the house. She'll call you madam and you just call everyone by their names. They will do anything you ask.*

*–Gee, I don't know what I'll do with myself.*

*–Oh, well, there'll be plenty to do with the wedding coming up.*

She feels herself redden.

*–You know what I wish for, Phil?*

*–No, but I'm going to get you an engagement ring. Something really beautiful that you can wear forever, and remember how happy you've made me.*

*–That's terrific! I didn't expect that! I'm so happy, Phil.*

*–What else do you wish for?*

She's quiet. She looks down at her tiny fingers and holds them in her strong hand. She will wear the ring on her right hand.

*–I wish that we become a family. A family with a mother and a father, and that we love our children and give them everything my brother Meyer and I never had.*

*–Gee, Bert, darling! I hope I can make your wish come true, because that's my wish too.*

Sounds that Bertha cannot recognise fill the night. Crickets throb insistently and frogs that sound like small monsters croak in the gutters near the window. Dogs bark in the distance. She can hear how far away they are. She thinks she also hears cattle, and beyond that people talking and singing. Phil takes her hands in his. He holds them as if he has received something he only ever thought he might dream of in fleeting images. Then he smiles and reaches over to a drawer on a side table.

*–Now, here's a little something for you. Some of these have been waiting for a while.*

He takes out a pile of correspondence from home that must contain thousands of words. *Oh my*, she says. There are four thick letters from Meyer, bless his heart, four from Gerty, her name and address typed on the envelope, one from Michael Sharlitt, one from Jack Girick, and a postcard from Gainor Jackson.

*–Are you happy, darling Bert?*

*–Yes! And boy, am I glad to hear from home. Thank you. This is grand!*

Phil puts on an opera record, and some passionate Italian pours his soul into the African night. Phil hands her a letter opener and leaves his young wife-to-be to reconnect with everything she's left and holds dear.

She opens the letters carefully. She already has their preservation in mind. Each line she reads will outlast her. Seventy-five years from this day, the pages and the words on them will emerge into the light, immediate, pertinent, the ink as real as it was to her in that pivotal moment.

Dear Bert,

I'm not sure whether this is my fourth letter or not but you'll be able to find out where it belongs by looking at the date.

At this writing you are only a few days away from the country where you'll find all the happiness you'll ever need. (Take it from me …) I've already become used to the idea of coming home from work, eating my dinner and not having your pleasant voice say to me while I am sitting in my armchair near the radiator, writing letters or doing H.W, 'Any mail, Meyer.' Don't think for one second that I don't miss you, because I am always thinking of you and you don't have to worry about not seeing me until I am old and gray, because in a short while, I'll show my freckled face in sunny Africa ...

With all my love, Meyer

P.S. You can even have the love I used to reserve for Helen. Are you getting a lot of mail. I imagine your fanmail is terrific.

✡

Middelburg itself is not exactly a gateway to the world. Still, this is where people shop and where they meet. Here, Bertha is introduced to some of Phil's extended family. He has eight siblings, including Aunt Dora. Bertha's family is now larger than she could have ever dreamed.

In the days to come, as she breathes in the smells of Africa and wonders whether she will ever grow accustomed to the semi-naked band of native children around the house, Phil senses his wife's disorientation. He tells Bertha she can help out at the general store if she likes. Her tiny fingers are a point of keen interest to native customers, which makes her self-conscious about using her hands at all. And she doesn't have the capacity to navigate the sea of foreign languages: Zulu, Afrikaans and Tswana conversations wash over her at the counter.

*–Sa'ubona! Kunjani. Ngiyafuna ...*
*–Goeie dag, mevrou. Het julle ...?*
*–Dumela Mma, o tsogile jang?*

✡

*March 12*
*The veld is very lonely at night. There are many cattle, sheep, goats and chickens.*

*March 13*
*Can't sleep. I have a lovely room. Philip gave me his room.*

She lies awake and ponders her life. At night, Africa closes in around the house and bathes her in its foreignness. It smells like wild animals and sweat. Nightbirds shriek and, far away in the Olifants River, hippos grunt. Distant drumming and singing are a reminder that the African people, who walk meekly about the house during the day in the roles of servants, are living another life away from the gaze of the white man. The sound of that life is unsettling. It speaks to her of ancient rhythms, and power, and – at a subterranean level – of unrest.

A spider the size of a human hand sits up in the corner of the room. Bertha has to get Phil in to catch it in a container. A cup is too small. They have to use a china bowl to get the intruder out of the bedroom. The hours creep towards midnight.

In the morning, all the heaviness of the night is banished by the radiance of the sun. The roosters crow from the chickenhouse rooftop. Cattle low and the piet-my-vrou bird announces the clear blue day ahead.

*March 17*
*We plan to have our wedding on June 12 1938.*

Esther is her favourite cousin. They play tennis together and share tales of high adventure. She adores Bertha and tells her she looks like a movie star.

*–I tell you, there are some of my aunts who are jealous of you, cousin*

*Bertha. Not my ma, Dora, but you know, Rosie and those older sisters of Phil. (Yes, there were really nine children!) Anyway, you just ignore them, see? You are the most gorgeous girl in the world and people will envy you.*

*–Esther, you're a darling and I'll always remember how kind you've been to me right from the beginning.*

*–I think you're really brave coming out here from so far away to live in the bushveld. Do you miss home much?*

*–Yep. Sometimes real bad.*

✡

*April 10*
*Eleven years since my late mother died. Today I have put a lit candle in memory of her blessed soul. I still miss her very much. Thank God she has stood over to watch Meyer and me.*

Eleven years have passed since Jacob Frank awoke and found his family's life changed forever. For Bertha, sometimes, the hollow shape of an absent mother is unbearable. Grief emerges unexpectedly in the spaces left behind by laughter, or in the moments before a sunrise. It creeps into the tiny day-to-day happenings that will never be shared, the kiss that will never be planted on a daughter's tear-streaked cheek, the thoughts and hopes and dreams of a young bride-to-be who would like to be a mother one day. In her heart, where she cherishes snippets of memories that speak of a mother's love, there are pictures of a parallel life, a family, that could have been.

✡

On the other side of the world, in a rented room in an apartment in Chicago, Jacob gathers his hat, his coat and his violin.

As he leaves the building, he fumbles in his pocket and takes out a worn calendar to make sure of the time he must be at the big house on Lake Michigan. He holds his breath. The day of loss.

The violin lessons he gives on his day off are a necessity – not just for the money they bring, but also for the gift of lightness that comes from losing himself in his student's musical progress.

Eleven years. In the early hours of April the tenth, eleven years ago, while he lay in the deepest part of his sleep, Ethel, Bertha and Meyer were his own for the last time.

He looks up at the white sky. In the weak sunlight of the half-hearted Illinois spring, he prays that his daughter has found happiness – that on this day, her heart will not be as heavy as his.

✡

On April 11, 1969, at four am South African time, which in America is still the evening of the tenth, exactly forty-two years after my great-grandmother Ethel's death, I take my first breath in Hillbrow, a suburb in the centre of Johannesburg. By the time I am twenty, Hillbrow will have the spectacular title of being the most violent place on earth.

I come into the world too soft for the rough nurses, the noise and bright lights. As is customary, this baby is quickly taken away from her twenty-year-old mother and bathed in cold water.

Within days I fear the loss of my mother and I cannot stay warm.

I will be the child whose lips go blue at the slightest suggestion of cool weather. I will cling to my mother. My fist will close around her finger and I will hold her hostage for hours each night while she sings and soothes and comforts me to sleep.

As a toddler, I will demand that my many dolls be wrapped, one after the other, in tight-fitting blankets, to keep them safe. When the blankets aren't smooth enough, or tight enough, I will dissolve in inconsolable tears.

I come into the world on the anniversary of my great-grandmother's death – and in my blood flows a legacy of whispers.

✡

When Bertha lights a candle to the memory of her beloved mother on April 10, 1938, she imagines what it would feel like to look back on a childhood that was bathed in a mother's love. If her mother had been alive, she wonders whether she would ever have considered coming to Africa.

✡

For Pesach, Bertha and Phil take a trip to Johannesburg. Pink and white cosmos flowers bend their petalled heads on the side of the road in the rush of passing cars.

Phil's mother has a ferocious hold on life. Though her body is failing, her eyes latch on to the willowy girl who comes through the front door. When Bertha walks in, the old lady is in her chair, covered with a mohair blanket. What delicacy, the old lady thinks. What beauty! She is ashen, as though she has seen an apparition. Bertha smiles and rushes to embrace her new mother-in-law. The old lady's mouth opens, but words fail her.

Outside, the deep skies stretch into eternity. Egyptian ibises call loudly to the earthbound humans below.

In the golden afternoon at Phil's parents' house, a small package, recently delivered and wrapped with string, lies on the front porch. Bertha and Phil finish cups of strong tea, and he leads her outside.

*–I believe this is what you've been waiting for, darling.*

*–What is it, Phil?*

At that moment a car pulls into the long gravel drive, and as Bertha looks up, she catches the eye of the driver. His gaze is immediately disapproving. She swallows her annoyance at his untimely arrival and looks back down at the parcel, before the company climbing out of the car demands her attention. Cousin Mildred is the first to emerge, followed by another of Phil's sisters – Rose, whom Bertha has never met – along with Yetta Mae and her little daughter, Bubbles.

Another of many family gatherings: a convergence of lives and destinies. As Joshua languidly steps out of his car and hitches his trousers, Bertha turns back to Phil. She unwraps the parcel to find a box with a gold lid, which she lifts with unsteady fingers. The facets of the diamonds capture and shatter the South African sunlight.

*–Oh, Phil. It's gorgeous. It's everything I could have dreamed of. I wish I'd been there when they packed it. It's almost too much to bear. Thank you!*

He wraps his arms around her waist and lifts her off her feet, and she kisses him quickly on the lips.

*–Well, well, I hope we're not interrupting.*

Bertha draws back from Phil. She sees Joshua's sardonic smile and critical gaze, and wants to hate him for being so rude.

Instead she holds out her good hand and cradles the diamond ring in her palm.

*–Isn't it just the most beautiful ring?* she says.

Joshua gives a curt nod and heads into the house, indicating with his thumb over his shoulder. *Ask the ladies, they'll give you the answer you're looking for.*

✡

One day, far in the future, when Granny Bee is in her seventies, living in a small flat in Johannesburg, and I am studying English at university, she will take me to her dressing table and unceremoniously pull out a wooden jewellery box. In the hazy mid-morning light, she will rummage through a few shiny brooches and strands of pearls, and pull out two rings and an old bible with my great-grandmother's name inscribed in it.

*–Darling, I just want to give these to you now. I want you to have them, and I want to be sure you get them before anything happens. They have a lot of sentimental value.*

*–Gran, thanks, but … but nothing's going to happen to you. You don't have to give these away.*

*–I want you to have them now and keep them always. This is a ring made of garnets that your grandpa Phil gave me for my birthday, and this is my engagement ring. The diamonds are real. The ring's platinum. It was a symbol of our love and all our hopes. See, over here is where we had it widened because I ate so much when I arrived that my fingers got fat between the buying and the wearing of the ring! And this old bible my dad gave me when he visited us at the orphanage. Some day you might understand why these things are important to me.*

I know that when I hug her she understands she can trust me to hold on to her treasures.

*–Thanks, Gran.*

I will carry them all over the world. The rings will be kept in a box in my bedroom in South Africa, while I finish my degree and fall blindly in love with a young musician who was once a soldier in a pointless war. In my small apartment in America's Midwest, I will take out the engagement ring and look at the South African diamonds when I'm sick and fighting for my breath every day; I will marvel at the narrowness of the ring, which I can barely fit on my baby finger.

In Australia, in the winter of 2013, I will read Bertha's diary. When I come across her entry about the engagement ring, I take it out of its box in the bathroom drawer. I hold the diamonds in the sunshine while rainbow lorikeets fight for the best position on the birdfeeder and scatter seeds all over the deck.

✡

Aunts, uncles, cousins and children assemble in the living room and on the verandah, and Phil slips the ring onto Bertha's finger in full view of everyone. She cannot believe she is now connected to each one of these people. While there is much admiration of her new ring, and of her beautiful clothes, her hat, her smile, her elegance, there are also emerging shadows: the brooding presence in the corner of the dining room; and the demeanour of Rose, who introduces herself to Bertha with a cool nod and a detectably insincere welcome.

For a few moments, Bertha doesn't understand Rose's words, but then they explode painfully inside her as their meaning reveals itself.

*–While your dress is gorgeous, darling, it's hardly the kind of thing you need for the life you'll be living out there. Oh, and I hear you speak no Afrikaans or African languages. That's not going to be much help to Phil or the family business. You're not exactly how Phil described you. I hope he can get over his disappointment.*

Bertha stumbles backwards. Nausea overwhelms her. She hears Rose continue to chatter on to other relatives. It's unbelievable. To top it all, in less than minutes, this woman seems to have taken on the role of wedding arranger. Phil does nothing to stop his sister. Bertha feels she might be sick. While everyone is caught up in conversation, she slips out through the dining room. She hurries past a maid in a chequered uniform who says *hello madam*, and into the backyard, where the full sun beats down on a washing line and dries flapping white pillowcases.

Giant cumulus clouds travel overhead, and beyond them, the sky is the colour of space, so blue that she imagines she can see stars in its depth. Roosters crow in the distance and, far to the west, clouds are developing into an uncharacteristic autumn storm. She feels faint and walks towards a small table next to a birdfeeder in the middle of the garden. She leans against it with her back to the house, kicking off her shoes. In front of her, the carpet of kikuyu grass spreads outward to the split-pole fence, and she can hear children laughing and chasing each other at the front of the house. She closes her eyes.

*–You have to ignore her behaviour, Bertha.*

A shadow crosses the sun. Her eyes fly open. He is so tall she has to bend her head backwards to meet his gaze. When she does, all her cultivated hatred of him dissolves. His azure eyes have gone from ice to fire. Her soul ignites. The heat is frightening, unfamiliar. She doesn't know her tears have left a smudged trail down her left cheek, until he takes another step closer and, resting his fingers on her temple, runs his thumb along her cheekbone.

–*What?* Her mouth is dry.

*–It's just her envy. All their envy. How can they have anything but disdain for a young American beauty who has entered their world, stolen a favourite brother's heart, and has the attention of every other man, woman and child in the house this afternoon?*

He is standing so close she can feel the warmth of his body. He is everything Phil is not: arrogant, rude, selfish, imposing – and charismatic. She takes a deep breath and tries to still her pulse.

–*What's bothering you, really, Bee?* He speaks softly, his breath on her cheek. She is in danger of losing herself. For a terrifying moment she imagines he will kiss her. She summons up annoyance.

*–Well, it's disgusting how everyone seems to think my wedding is theirs to organise. I certainly miss my own family. My brother, my father, my late mother, my best friend …*

*–You don't have to do this, you know.*

*–Do what?*

*–Marry Phil, as I've said.*

*–One thing you don't know about me, Mr Lourie, is that when I give my word, it's a promise. God is my witness, and I would rather die than break such a promise.*

A clap of thunder makes both of them look skyward.

*–You might do well to take a less fanatical stance on your idea of a promise. Your life is a valuable thing and I'd hate to see you throw it away, as I might have mentioned before. I hope you've considered your own happiness, and whether love is part of the equation.*

The sun vanishes. The smell of ozone fills the air. Lightning flickers. She slips away from Joshua Lourie, scraping her arm against the table. His usually disdainful expression is gone; his cheeks are flushed. She folds her deformed hand tightly in her other, so that her new engagement ring flashes brilliantly.

*–Well, I beg your pardon, Mr Lourie! Phil is my future husband. There is no one who can ever love me as much as he does!*

As she turns her back on him and walks to the house, Joshua's words hang heavy in the air behind her: *Don't be so sure.*

✡

Life in this new land begins to take on a recognisable form. Perhaps, she thinks, she might get used to the maids and gardeners, the constant murmur of incomprehensible African languages. The servants do indeed keep the house spotless and Bertha treats them kindly; but, at his behest, she takes on Phil's disposition: one cannot afford these natives the sense that they are a white person's equal. It is important to be the *madam,* and if possible learn some Afrikaans, Zulu or Tswana.

In the evenings, Phil returns from work at the store. The sound of his car crushing the stony drive, chickens squawking as they rush out of the way, is as uplifting as a symphony. During the day she has too much time to think, but she tries to keep busy with wedding plans. Each afternoon, a deathly stillness descends on the highveld. Even the distant dogs stop barking. Flies buzz lazily against the windows and die in the crevices between the glass and the ledge. The servants all go to sleep. Sometimes Phineas sleeps sitting straight up against the whitewashed wall at the back of the house. The air smells like smoke and dust.

Within days all the green has vanished. Autumn has come, they say, along with its absence of rain, and the rust-coloured grass reaches towards an empty sky.

The second hand on the clock ticks loudly and slowly from the living room. These are the hard hours. The long hours. Into such portions of time comes nostalgia for the past: Bertha longs for her brother, and brings up memories of Gertrude and the home and Jack Girick and Michael Sharlitt and Al. The loneliness of being an outsider in the bushveld is sometimes more than she can bear.

But then, as evening approaches, the cares of the day dissolve. Now are the moments that become treasures, filled with all the potential of the future. Phil worships her. He has brought her across the world and rescued her from obscurity.

He bursts into the house with a cheery hello and an arm full of pink roses. He holds her tightly to him and kisses her on the lips, banishing the dusty thoughts of the hot afternoon.

The sun grows huge and red, like a giant egg sitting on the grassy edge of the world. The verandah looks out over the plains of Africa.

Phil's happy mood is contagious; he showers her with compliments and promises of what life will hold, and she frames these in her heart, and believes in them.

*April 20*
*Philip and I spend many wonderful evenings together. I have grown very fond of him and I am sure I love him very much.*

*April 21*
*Received a letter from Gertrude Fogelson, wrote that Meyer is messenger boy at Lamples.*

✡

Phil is sometimes at a loss. During his hours at work he wants to get home; he worries that Bertha might decide to return to America if she finds her life here too empty.

With the wedding only two months away, trips to Johannesburg are planned. The first one is to celebrate their engagement and make a formal occasion of it. The party, which coincides with the seder, is a joyous one, but there is a stain on this page of her life. Every word that Rose breathes is designed to get Bertha off her high American horse.

*April 24*
*Nothing of importance today. Only I feel that now I can't seem to get adjusted to some people that live here. They have a gruesome sarcastic nature and they think they are humorous but they hurt my feelings badly ...*

✡

Letters pour into Groblersdal (via Middelburg) from America. Meyer Frank misses his sister; he tells her that life is hunky dory. His pay as a messenger boy is pretty okay. In fact, if only their dad could get a decent job, Meyer writes, everything would be perfect. Gertrude, who admits that she's had a crush on Al for years, wishes he would ask her to marry him, because if he doesn't, or if he does something stupid like go over to Europe to fight in the war, she's going to agree to Leon Weiner. Bertha tries to write replies that elucidate her life in Africa and do justice to the African bushveld. She tells of how an African woman was eaten by a crocodile while fetching water from the banks of the Olifants River. She herself hasn't seen any lions yet, but the other day there were zebras grazing near the roadside, and a cobra was found in a tree near the house. Luckily Phineas – houseboy, cook and gardener – chopped off its head with a shovel.

The weather has begun to cool. At night, frost turns the elephant grass white, but the days are warm and bright. Sunsets are a blaze of chaos that vanish into sudden dark. Proximity to the equator means that twilight is brief. The night skies are littered with billions of stars and mornings are announced by deep-throated louries and high-flying hadadas. She never dreamed that the world could be such a wild and beautiful place. She writes this to Gertrude, to Jack Girick, and sends an extended version to Michael Sharlitt, telling him of her wedding date and plans.

✡

On her next trip to Johannesburg, Bertha meets the wedding-dress designer. There are long chats with her bridesmaids-to-be about the colours and materials of every dress and ribbon. She discovers with relief that Rose is out of town for the duration of this visit.

In the evenings, sitting in the living room with her future mother-in-law, Bertha leafs through the family albums. Here's Phil as a baby. Here he is again, two years old. He was such a darling right from the start. Here is the youngest boy, Jack. He died three years ago of pneumonia, which broke his mother's heart. And here is Phil again, always caring, always the kind one. Of all the children, he is now the centre of his mother's universe.

Bertha looks at the woman who gave birth nine times and had to see her own child die before her. Her body has been sacrificed to love, but also to grief – that much is evident. Bertha is glad her presence seems to afford the old lady so much pleasure.

But sadness creeps in. All these children have grown up with a mother. Phil had someone to wrap her arms around him when he cried after scraping the skin off his knee. When he came home filthy and covered in grass and mud, there was someone to tell him to clean his shoes and not track dirt into the house. When his heart ached for a girl in America he'd never met, his mother's heart ached with him. The void in Bertha's life is an abyss. She looks into it and cannot see the bottom. She feels adrift and fights to keep back tears.

*May 25*
*I am spending a few weeks in Jo'burg and getting acquainted with my new mom and father. Poor darling, so sick and loves her Philip so much. She often relates about Philip when as a little baby he was so lovely. A mother's love is the truest and what love I missed from my beloved mother. My brother Meyer and I shared that.*

*May 29*
*Going shopping for wedding gown. I had it designed the way I have always wanted it to be … it looks very effective and beautiful. Philip paid 35 dollars seven pounds … I had a 4.5 length veil and my wreath*

*was made of white feathers. My bouquet of Arum lillies was flown from Capetown … my flower girl is Bubbles Ethel Smith. Her dress is just like mine and she looked so cute.*

*June 1*
*During the morning Phil and I went down to the Rabbi and signed our marriage license.*

*I'm rather thrilled being a bride because it is one grand event … Yes. I am very happy. Only two dear people whom I wished to come to my wedding. My belated beloved mother and brother.*

Preparations for the wedding are in full force, in both Johannesburg and Groblersdal. The bridesmaids are bees surrounding a flower. With her slim figure, laughing blue eyes, thick curly hair and movie-actress accent, she is an enviably perfect bride.

Even Mildred is cheerful and excited. She says to her cousin one afternoon: *Joshua calls you Bee. Is that okay with you?*

Yetta Mae decides it's a brilliant idea.

–*Bee sounds great,* she says. *I'm going to call you that, cousin Bee. Do you mind?*

–*No, that's all right. I don't mind.*

So Bertha becomes Bee to her South African cousins. It seems odd that the term originates with the arrogant Joshua Lourie.

As she spends time with Mildred, she imagines what it might feel like to be engaged to such a man. Certainly he is handsome. But he is also frightening. It knots her stomach to think of the way he looks at her, to remember the touch of his finger on her face. To know that he could do that while engaged to be married fills her with righteous anger on her cousin's behalf. At the same time, her mouth dries out when she thinks of him, and her heart races.

The cousins go off to play tennis at the Johannesburg Country and Tennis Club on a Saturday morning when Phil and Bertha are in town on one of their weekend visits. Encouraged by her success at deck tennis on the ship, Bertha is an enthusiastic participant. The luminous green lawns of the tennis club are peppered with birds. The sounds of nature are louder than any human noise and Bertha marvels at the subtropical beauty of her surroundings. There is no sign of the dissonance to come; at least, not to the casual observer. To know the future would require a deep listening to the wind and the birdsong, a keen vision that would see the restlessness in the whispering, bending grass.

While playing tennis, Bertha exerts herself and her cheeks turn bright red. Cousin Esther beats her. Everyone laughs, but she feels ill.

She will not discover for another twenty years that she has a congenital heart defect; an inherited heartache.

The men arrive to have drinks. Phil looks dashing in his suit and Bertha is proud of him. His friend George is a charmer and kisses Bertha's hand before ordering drinks for everyone. Joshua Lourie arrives sometime later. His imposing figure is impossible to miss as he walks across the lawn to join the other men. Noting how he specifically ignores her, she chats to Esther. She can tell, however, that he finds his companions insufferable.

Joshua's intolerance makes Phil miserable after half an hour. He walks out to find Bertha laughing with Esther and doesn't want to interrupt them. When a crowd of friends and relatives arrive for lunch at the club, no one notices that, by then, neither Bertha Frank nor Joshua Lourie is part of the group.

✡

She is standing beneath the wide branches of a syringa tree. Her short tennis skirt reveals smooth legs which are now golden brown.

Her cheeks are pink and she is mildly out of breath; her heart is working harder than it should.

His hair looks disorderly and his eyes are restless. The two of them are screened from the tennis club by a thick hedge.

–*I have to talk to you*, he says.

–*I don't understand*, she replies, her eyes flickering to the voices and laughter to her left.

He runs his hands through his hair several times.

–*I can't bear thinking about you giving yourself to Phil. It's driving me to distraction, Bee. Since I first set eyes on you, I've wanted you for myself. Tell me*, he says, suddenly reaching out his hands to run them over her arms and draw her closer, *tell me that you feel nothing for me, that you hate me, detest my vile manners, my lack of self-control and the fact that I'm engaged to your cousin. Just say the words.*

Bertha is dumb. Her heart feels as though it's in her throat. He pulls her up against him. She shakes, a leaf tumbled across the desert by a dust-devil. And then he bends his head and kisses her long and full on the lips.

Midday. Time slows to nothing with the sun directly overhead. Their shadows are small circles at their feet. A dove calls to its mate from the branches above. Sweat runs down her spine and her stomach, and she puts her hands on his chest, and pushes him away.

–*You don't want to, do you?* His voice is a harsh whisper.

–*I'm going to marry Phil, Mr Lourie! Please get away from me!*

He wraps her left hand in both of his and holds it between them to his heart. And then he lets her go, his eyes red and shimmering.

–*Yes, of course. And I will marry your cousin Mildred and we'll all live out our days in the most mediocre way possible. For a moment there, kissing you, I almost thought we had changed the universe.* His words fall like cold pebbles into an empty water tank and ricochet inside her heart.

*–They'll be looking for me. I've got to go!*

*–I'll tell you something, Bee, and this I will keep as my secret and solace for the rest of my life. You didn't act like a girl madly in love with her fiance accosted by an insufferable stranger. No. For an eternal second, we were one.*

✡

Bertha makes it back to the tennis club and Joshua disappears for the rest of the afternoon. No one seems to give it a moment's thought. Phil catches a glimpse of her and makes his way to her side, a cool drink in his hand.

*–Where were you, darling? I've been looking for you everywhere!*

*–I had to go outside. It was stuffy in here.*

*–Tennis tires you out too much. Did you beat Esther?*

*–No, but I did beat Yetta Mae and Mildred.*

*–You're becoming a real tennis pro. Would you like something to eat?*

*–No, thank you.*

*–What about this drink?*

*–No, thank you. I'm not really thirsty, or hungry.*

He's at a loss. She can't help him. Her mind is in disarray. She has to put everything that just happened away from her and make sure that Joshua Lourie and his words are forever outside of her thoughts. She tries to look at Phil's face, but she cannot do it.

At dinner that night, Bertha is quieter than usual. She goes to sleep in the comfortable room smelling of floor polish, which her future in-laws have provided, and prays that in the morning she will be feeling as a joyful bride-to-be should feel.

Sunshine seeps in beneath the heavy curtains, and when she opens them, a glorious blue day full of hope lies unblemished before her. As she opens the door, she finds a note on the polished corridor floor:

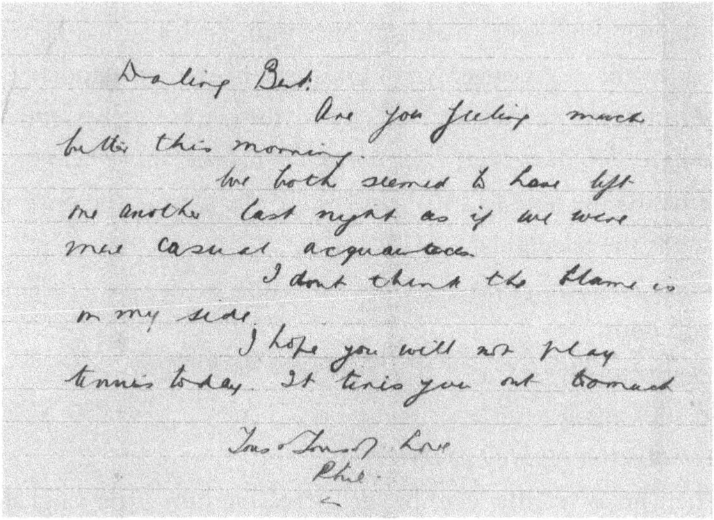

Darling Bert:
Are you feeling much better this morning.
We both seemed to have left one another last night as if we were mere casual acquaintances.
I dont think the blame is on my side.
I hope you will not play tennis today. It tires you out too much

Tons o Tons of Love
Phil.

✡

At breakfast, Bertha looks at Phil's kind face, at his hands, and she smiles when he looks up to find her watching him.

–*What are you staring at, my dear?*

–*At the man I'm going to marry.*

–*Do you love him? The man you're going to marry?* he asks. By his grin anyone can tell that he knows what the answer will be.

–*Well, I'm sure I do,* she says. She leans across the boiled eggs in egg-cups, something she's never seen before in America, and knocks hers over. Then she kisses Phil, so that he closes his eyes and eventually pulls away.

–*You shouldn't play cruel games, young lady. Any more of that and I'll be in trouble. And so will you!*

She blushes and laughs – a young woman learning slowly about the unspoken currents that run between men and women and take them to places she has never been.

✡

The June wind off Lake Michigan bites into Jacob's face as he makes his way to the city centre. Mrs Goldstein, his current landlady, has helped him translate his long Yiddish note into short English sentences. *Bertha and Phil. Mazel tov. Long life and happiness. Your Daddy.*

He hands the note to a woman behind the glass at the post office who sends the telegrams.

–*Your daughter's getting married?* she says.

Jacob nods.

–*In Africa?*

He nods again.

–*Too bad you couldn't be there.*

When he leaves, his eyes burn. Incredible how little English he needs: everyone seems to have enough words to make up for the ones he lacks.

✡

The wedding is everything she dreamed a wedding might be. Her dress is exactly as she imagined. Oh, if only Gert were here to share this! And her precious Meyer, and her father, and her late mother, and everyone at the home.

On this day in June, the skies arc overhead, the deepest colour she has ever seen. The breeze plays with the leaves in the gutter outside the synagogue, and her bridesmaids lift her long train so that it doesn't touch the ground. Uncle Woolf's arm is shaking as much as hers as he links it through hers and whispers, *Your mother is smiling in heaven at you, darling Bee.*

Her eyes are filled with tears of happiness and heartbreak. Next to her is the warm presence of her own uncle, her mother's brother. He connects her to her roots and takes her to meet her future.

June 12, 1938.

Bertha Frank marries Phil Davidow.

He looks terribly handsome in his top hat and tails, and she is overwhelmed with pride. The traditional Jewish ceremony happens in Berea, near the centre of Johannesburg. The pole-bearers and the wedding guests – everyone except Uncle Woolf and Phil – are a blur to Bertha. She is the happiest person on earth.

The first part of the ceremony is the kiddushin. Here, Phil gives Bertha a ring of eternal commitment, made of platinum. This prohibits his bride to every other man. During the chuppah the couple stand beneath the canopy as their pathway together begins. Phil breaks the glass with his right foot, symbolising the destruction of Jerusalem, a reminder to all that joy in life is tempered with grief.

*Mazel tov* rings out around the crowd, and Bertha emerges into the sunlight, on the arm of her new husband.

In the dances that follow, someone plays *Hava Nagila* on an old violin and tears run down Bertha's cheeks.

She throws her garter at Phil's friend George, and he goes bright red. When she throws her bouquet, she aims it straight into the waiting arms of Mildred Braker.

As they leave the synagogue, a cloud covers the sun, and a burst of rain and confetti shower the newlyweds. Dora remarks:

*–An omen of everlasting good luck, my darlings, mazel tov to you!*

Bertha wants to record every moment, every second of her life at this time. She will never forget any part of it. Consumed by the hustle and bustle of wedding preparations, she has left her diary empty for all of June. But she has kept every event in her head, so that later, as the newlyweds travel north towards Mozambique for their honeymoon, she will commit those memories to paper.

After the wedding, the bride and groom change and meet their guests at a generous reception. On this occasion, Rose has masked her jealousy and plays the devoted sister to Phil.

Bertha is overwhelmed when none other than Harold, her dear shipmate, arrives to wish her mazel tov. Having him here at this moment makes her somehow sad, and yet she treasures his presence. He is the memory of a journey bursting with hope and possibility, when life might have gone in any direction. At this moment in time, though, the direction is set, and she can see flickers of anguish – or is it regret? – in his kind hazel eyes.

–*My dear Bertha, you are the most beautiful bride in the world,* he says. *I hope you will be happy always.*

–*Harold, you have no idea how much this means to me! You're the only friend from my past who I can actually call my own!*

–*Hey hey hey,* says George, Phil's friend, *no hogging the bride!*

–*Stay who you are, Bert. And remember …*

–*Shipmates forever,* she says.

–*Just what I was about to say.*

*My Wedding Day*
*Today. My wedding! It was held at the Berea Synagogue. My happiest day of my life.*

*Dressed in a white gown I feel like a queen. The wedding, a lovely ceremony, the cantor singing the chanted wedding hymns. Philip looks marvelous in his tails and top hat. Very handsome. I walked down the aisles trembling, my arm in Uncle Woolf's. Oh! God how sad and happy I am. The lovely ceremony with Philip's mother and father looking on. Phil placed the eternal band of life together on my wedded finger, a lovely platinum. We are married. After Philip broke the glass under the canopy we have become husband and wife. I am now Mrs. Philip Davidow …*

*The only friend I had was my ship mate Harold Feldman came to see me. I really thought this was some wonderful gesture. I'll never forget him.*

On their wedding night, Bertha lies in her new husband's arms. For the first time, she is in a bed with another human being. Every bride, she thinks, waits for this. The anticipation makes her breathless, terrified. She so wishes she will not be disappointed. The idea of doing something she has barely imagined is enough to put her into a near state of shock. She thinks she must be the most innocent and protected young woman she knows.

When the sun's morning rays pierce through the bottom of the curtain, she wakes up and looks at the man next to her. How strange to have done what they did! Nothing was as she expected. She's disturbed by this loneliness and dissatisfaction. Is that it? That is what poets and song-writers and romance-writers, through the ages and all the movies, have been holding up as the ultimate joy, the ultimate union between a man and a woman? It feels so strange to be on the other side of this experience. She sighs and Phil opens a tired eye and smiles.

*–Lourenço Marques, here we come*, he says. *Bertha Davidow, have I told you what a darling you are to me?* His arm slips around her waist and he pulls her right against him, kissing her. She grins beneath his lips and laughs, pushing his naked chest away from her.

*–I believe you have. Several times! All night, in fact.*

*–That's because I don't want you to ever forget it.*

*–I won't*, she says, wriggling away from him. *Now, Phil, you stop that! We have to get ready. The train's leaving at nine!*

✡

The train rolls out of Johannesburg towards Mozambique. As the city vanishes behind them, they find themselves plunging through bush that thickens with every passing minute. Soon the dry air is tempered with humidity, and the wintry Transvaal landscape has given way to the tropics. Fertile earth nourishes trees and people alike. In the shade of enormous leaves and canopies, African children sit and wave at the passing train. In some areas, as the train slows down, the little kaffirs, as Phil calls them, run alongside the carriages and beg for sweets or coins.

Mozambique is a Portuguese colony. But long before Vasco da Gama explored its fecund beauty in 1498, the Bantu people lived there, trading and making their lives from the first century CE. Eventually, the millions of Mozambicans, tired after five hundred years of colonial rule, will rebel against the Portuguese and, in 1975, will win it back.

Then, a civil war will rage across the land, lasting for twenty years, littering the earth with landmines that will kill thousands of children and leave thousands more without their limbs. In the next century, 80 per cent of the population will live in extreme poverty. It will no longer be South Africa's number one honeymoon destination.

When Bertha looks out of the train window, they are travelling through orchards outside Lourenço Marques. She has never seen oranges grow and she cannot believe her eyes. As far as the eye can see, golden citrus globes hang like miniature suns in the dense green. The air is aromatic as it pours through the window.

Beyond the orchards, the land opens out somewhat, and there are antelope grazing. She sees a zebra, and then, as if in a dream, a group of three giraffe.

*–Phil, look over there! It's a giraffe!*

*–Well, three to be exact, darling Bert.*

He laughs at her wide-eyed wonder. One giraffe is close enough that the passing train makes him turn his elegant neck and blink with long, lazy eyelashes at this interruption to his leafy snack.

*–I never imagined in my wildest dreams that I would travel so far from home and make my life here, Phil.*

*–I'm so glad you did. I hope your honeymoon is everything you can dream it to be. You've made my dreams come true. I love you, darling!*

*June 13*
*The train is rolling on to Lourenzo Marques four hundred miles from Jo'burg … Philip treats me so wonderfully and we have so much fun.*

The Polana Hotel overlooks the Indian Ocean. The beaches are unlike anything Bertha has ever seen – wide and white, disappearing beneath turquoise water. A distant wreck lies beneath circling seabirds.

Having never swum in an ocean before, it takes a while before she braves the surf with Phil, holding his hand. The water is warm and tugs at her. She laughs as it sucks at her feet, taking away the sand beneath them so that she sinks deeper; when she looks down, she's dizzy. She sways and Phil tips her so that she falls and he catches her, carrying her playfully into water that is waist deep. Never, in all her life, has she had so much fun.

The days pass by in a haze. There are films and tennis matches and brightly coloured colonial houses to feast her eyes upon in Lourenço Marques. Their days are replicas of the lives of lazy millionaires. She could get used to this, she thinks.

Walking down at the docks one afternoon, Bertha spies a ship that reminds her of the *Dunbar Castle*. She and Phil run down to the port, and they are stunned to see that it is indeed the ship that brought her to South Africa.

They speak to some of the sailors on the gangplank, and soon they are boarding the ship and entering the first-class lounge, where Bertha, to her delight, meets many familiar faces.

–*This is my husband, Philip*, she tells the captain. *We've been married only a few days.*

–*May I congratulate you, my dear! What a handsome fellow you have found yourself. Is this the man you were going to meet for the first time in Cape Town?*

–*I am he*, says Phil, grinning. *The luckiest man alive.*

–*I'd say so. You're damned lucky she didn't get snapped up by some of the lurking sharks on board during our voyage. I'd say you have quite a catch there, Mr …?*

–*Davidow.* Bertha can feel herself blushing. She looks up at Phil, who grabs her hand and tucks it under his arm, pulling her closer.

–*Well, a pleasure to meet you, Mr Davidow, and Bertha, may good luck continue to follow you wherever you go and whatever you do.*

After meeting up with these old acquaintances, they leave the ship. In less than a year, the *Dunbar Castle* will hit a German mine at sea on its way from England to Mozambique. It will split in two and sink within fifteen minutes. Eight people will be unaccounted for. The captain himself and another crewmember will die.

✡

Sometimes, Phil annoys her. He hates having snaps taken. He's stubborn. He's used to doing things his way.

On the way back to their room after dinner, he asks her what she is thinking about.

–*I don't know*, she says. *I guess I was just wondering how old you'll be this year.*

–*I'll be thirty-two.*

–*Your mother said something about you turning thirty-four this year.*

–*What does it really matter, Bert?*

–*It doesn't! I'd just like to know your actual age.*

–*I told you.*

–*Ugh, Phil, you really get my goat.* She crosses her arms in front of her.

–*That's ridiculous. My mother's old. You can believe her or me.*

She decides to drop the matter. He is, after all, kind to a fault.

At night, in the moonlit luxury of their hotel room, white curtains billowing in the salty breeze, his love is a hunger that consumes him. She is sure she should feel something similar, something wild, but she doesn't understand his animal passion, which, if she must be honest, has taken a bit of getting used to. Nevertheless, she relishes the power she seems to have over him. As the nights progress, she learns that her hands, her lips, her smile, the way she moves can raise his temperature to burning hot, and this, in and of itself, is a revelation. She understands what he wants, and she knows it is hers to give, or to withhold.

✡

The journey from Lourenço Marques back to Johannesburg is a slow descent into despondency. The greenery thins and turns to yellow, then brown. The humidity drops and the cold dry air comes rushing through the train window, tasting of dust.

Aunt Dora is at the station to meet the returning honeymooners; she travels to Johannesburg every week to buy wholesale supplies for the store. Bertha hugs her tight as she fights the desire to sink into gloom. Smoky air from winter veld-fires makes her feel as if she has just arrived at the station at the end of the world.

✡

*July 4*
*The signing of Declaration of Independence today, and it certainly must be warm in US … I do get homesick but God is with me and knows what's the best.*

Her distance from America is conspicuous in the dry winter veld. Letters from Gert and Meyer are frequent and lift her spirits. She is especially touched by a long letter from Michael Sharlitt:

*Bellefaire*

**THE CLEVELAND JEWISH ORPHAN HOME**

*Fairmount and Belvoir Boulevards, Cleveland*

P. O. BOX 3564

FRED LAZARUS, JR., PRESIDENT
COLUMBUS, OHIO

MICHAEL SHARLITT
SUPERINTENDENT

September 8, 1938

Mrs. Philip Davidow
c/o Braker
Middleburg
Transvall, S. Africa

My dear Bertha:

That was a wonderful letter you wrote. It certainly takes a long time for mail to arrive. Your letter was dated August 7th. It got here Tuesday, September 6th.

Oddly enough, on the Sunday previous, September 4th, Jackie Davis was married in our chapel. Of course you remember him. There was quite a crowd out, especially of graduates.

It is so good to realize that you are so happy and when I say this, I have in mind the feelings of all of us. Somewhere, Bertha, you must have been blessed. I recall a few years back how discouraged you were, but you kept plugging patiently and faithfully and see how lovely everything has worked out.

I have an idea that if Meyer goes, he will give a very good account of himself. Meyer is a fine lad, one of the finest that we have had here. I haven't seen him recently. I believe he is still out of town, because when he is in Cleveland, he never fails to stop out at Bellefaire of a Sunday.

We have had a very happy summer. There were the usual picnics and hikes and activities in athletics. The weather was splendid most of the time. A considerable number of the children were away on vacations, some of them for the entire summer. All kept well, I am glad to say.

Most of the workers are back from their vacations. Mr. Girick left Wednesday night, August 31st. The graduates gave him a Testimonial Dinner at Hotel Hollenden which was well attended and quite a demonstration. His successor reported for duty this morning. I have just completed making the rounds with him. He seems to be a likeable young man and I am hoping the children will take to him.

County Fair, this year, was one of the most successful we ever had. The children took in about $350. That is a lot of money for a children's enterprise. The girls' handicraft attracted special attention. They had been making rugs and afghans and valuable single pieces. Their work has become a real feature.

-2-

Your description of the life of the natives is good and very interesting. I wish parts of your letter were more generally read by folks on the campus but I have to preserve the confidence of letter writing.

Yesterday the children went off to school. It was hard for me to see them go and as the busses left early yesterday morning for the first time, with the children looking so trim and attractive, I could not help but feel a pride in the privilege that is mine. It was a joy to see everybody looking so lovely. My own Joe is beginning senior high school. It is so hard to realize that he is no longer a baby.

You probably know that a number of our boys and girls go to high school in Cleveland; John Hay, Glenville and East Tech and one boy goes to Cleveland Trade School. We have only handful who go to Heights High now.

Rosh Hashonah will be with us on the 26th, Bertha. I want to wish you and your good husband and all of your people a very happy, healthful and successful New Year. I will be thinking of you when we are in the synagogue. All of us will have you in mind. I hope this finds you well. It is so good to feel that you are so very happy.

Sincerely,
Michael Sharlitt

Some days she accompanies Phil and Uncle Woolf in the store, but as a general rule, she stays at home. The Jewish New Year comes and goes. The newlyweds go to Johannesburg and Bertha sees all the films she has already seen in America, with Yetta Mae.

The Orthodox service is a foreign experience. She's used to a much more open, reformed approach to God and religion. In her heart she vows she will always be true to what she knows and the God who has been so good to her and sent her such a dear man to be her husband.

Meyer's nineteenth birthday goes by, and Bertha is not there to celebrate with him. She aches for the little boy he was, to have him near her and to share things with him. He writes at least twice a week, and that gives her solace, but it takes so very long for news to reach her.

And then, just before they leave Jo'burg to go home, Phil's mother tells Bertha:

*–You know, Bertha, it would be very good if you would pay old Mrs Lourie a visit before you go back home. She spent the Jewish New Year all on her own.*

Bertha finds her husband in the living room listening to the wireless and suggests the visit to him.

*–Well, that's a kind thought,* he says. *I'd be happy to take you there and leave you for an hour. Can't stay there, I'm afraid. She's almost as caustic as her son.*

*–Is she?*

*–Oh, she'll be sweet to you, darling, no doubt. Her sour-faced son was away on business and didn't ensure that she had someone to spend time with … even though we did invite her, you know. I'll take you as soon as the news is over.*

And this is how Bertha finds herself in the dining room of the house where Joshua Lourie spent his childhood. His mother wears a floral dress, and a severe grey bun on her head. She has her son's angular nose and fathomless blue eyes. After the first pleasantries are exchanged, and Mrs Lourie makes it clear that she appreciates the visit, they go into the parlour, where Mabel, the maid, is pouring tea.

*–Be a good girl and spare me the small talk, will you, Bertha dear? I'm too old to waste time talking about the weather and clothes and the latest gossip. I am interested in a few things, though. How is married life treating you?*

*–Very well, thank you.*

*–Good, good. And are you now well informed about the facts of life?*

Bertha flushes. She puts her teacup down with such unsteady fingers that hot tea spills into the saucer.

*–Well, I'm sure that's a yes, Mrs Lourie!*

*–One would hope so. I hope your husband knows what brings a woman pleasure, young lady. You know, so many men are just in it for themselves, if you'll pardon the pun.*

Bertha looks at the white light pouring through the frosted window of the entrance hall, searching for an escape from this most uncomfortable conversation.

*–Excuse me, Mrs Lourie, I have no idea what you're talking about. My husband takes care of me very well and we have a wonderful time together.*

*–Yes, yes and all that. Well, good luck to you, then. Are you planning to have a family?*

*–Yes, it's my dream.*

*–Of course. A family will fill your heart and become the ultimate pleasure. Nevertheless, I do feel sorry for you.*

*–I'm sure that's not necessary, Mrs Lourie! Why?*

*–Oh, you're so far away from all those you love … Do you miss them?*
It looks as though she wanted to say something different but thought better of it.

*–Of course I do.*

*–Life here must seem very barbaric to you, coming from such a glamorous place.*

*–I wouldn't exactly call Cleveland glamorous. I'm very happy with my decision, if that's what you mean.*

*–Yes, well, perhaps it is. Hmm. I think I hear a knock at the front door. Will you be so kind as to get it for me? My arthritis is playing up.*

Phil's early. He hasn't even been gone for thirty minutes. Perhaps, thankfully, he's changed his mind and come back for a cup of tea after all. She's had about as much of the old lady's pity as she can take. She goes over to the door and throws it open, a smile of relief on her face.

Only it's not Phil she's smiling at.

It's Joshua Lourie.

When Joshua Lourie appears at his mother's front door, he is holding a briefcase in his right hand and a violin case in his left. Bertha knows he is a businessman, but she is about to discover that he plays first violin in the Johannesburg Symphony Orchestra.

–*What are you doing here?* His eyes are accusatory. Her smile dissolves.

–*I came to visit your mother.*

–*I'm sure that's very kind of you, Bee, but don't you have more important things to attend to, now that you're married?*

–*I'll be leaving shortly. I heard your mother was all alone for the Jewish New Year and Phil's mother thought I should pay her a visit.*

–*So you're not here out of the kindness of your own heart, but out of some sense of misplaced duty.*

Bertha feels his coldness as a sharp pain in her stomach. Her eyes smart and she is on the verge of pushing past him and running into the street.

–*You're insufferably rude! I've done nothing to deserve your insults!* she bursts out, and tries to get past him. He blocks her way with his solid, dark-suited frame.

At that moment, she throws a lightning glance at his face and sees his eyes melt. He puts his violin and his briefcase down on the verandah.

–*God forgive me,* he says. *I … wasn't expecting to see you, Bee. You've caught me off guard.*

–*Is it necessary to be so rude?* She's surprised at how firm and cool her voice sounds when her whole body is outraged.

–*No, no, of course not. My God, Bertha, it's just that seeing you here … I didn't anticipate what that would do to me.* Faced with his contrition, her fury dissolves into something so disturbing that she has to wrest her eyes away from his face. *Please accept my apology. I'll behave in a civilised fashion from now on.*

A voice echoes through the house:

*–Joshua, is that you? I didn't expect you today. For heaven's sake, what's taking you so long at the door, Bertha? Mabel, another teacup, please, and another pot of tea! And hurry up, I've been left on my own for far too long!*

The rest of her time at Mrs Lourie's is most uncomfortable. Joshua just spends the time sipping his tea, and eyeing her shamelessly without saying a word. His mother becomes more and more obnoxious in her criticisms of life in the bushveld as opposed to the city, and Bertha is infinitely glad to hear the sound of Phil's car in the drive. As she leaps off her seat and hastily thanks her hosts, Joshua reaches into his pocket and pulls out some free tickets to the orchestra's performance that night. A wedding present, he says. He explains that he plays first violin for the orchestra, and his mother adds that they must come, as Joshua will be playing on this new purchase: a 200-year-old violin.

Bertha and Phil head back to Middelburg and do not attend the concert. But the sight of the violin has awoken memories in Bertha. On the way back to Groblersdal, Bertha does not see the winter veld, or the setting sun, or the orange sky. She hears the sound of her father's violin while her mother cooks chicken soup and boils cabbage in the kitchen. The room she is in is so dark she cannot make out the furniture, or remember what is in there, besides the two beds. The winter is so cold that the windows have frosted over on the inside, and she and Meyer flake pieces of ice off the glass and eat them. The sheep are noisy out the back, and sound like loud humans complaining. She is about seven. The memory emerges with a long-lost feeling of being whole, and wholly loved.

As she looks over at Phil with his hand firmly on the wheel, she touches his sleeve and leans her head on his shoulder. One thing is certain. Despite everything, she cannot deny that she has found someone who makes her feel loved.

✡

Phil's birthday is coming up and Bertha's still not quite sure of his age. Spring has arrived in the Transvaal. The rainclouds gathering overhead are so enormous that Bertha wonders whether she is hallucinating. Then, there is a crack of thunder, and another, and jagged forks of lightning split the sky. She senses that a force is about to be unleashed on the land.

As usual in the afternoons, she counts the hours until Phil's return. Chickens scratch in the yard and, somewhere, a dog barks. All the servants are asleep. Their children shriek in the courtyard at the back of the house, and then, at another rumble of distant thunder, go running down to the servants' quarters, where they live in close proximity to other families, sometimes sleeping five to a room, with a single mattress on the floor. Bertha doesn't know how one is supposed to get used to the way the natives live, but her relatives have assured her she will. Another flash of lightning sets her nerves on edge. There is much she cannot fathom about this country. She may never feel at home, she thinks. She doesn't know how she will get used to calling Anna a 'girl', when she is some years older than her. Black people all over the country are called 'girls' and 'boys', which puts them in their place as not quite adults, not quite capable of managing themselves, not quite equal to any adult white person. Despite this pervasive perspective, Bertha cannot help but see Anna and the native servants as they are: oppressed human beings working for a low wage on someone's rural property.

The wind whips up and the clouds consume the entire sky. A deafening crack sounds as white light flashes through the room, and a tree next to the house bursts into flame.

Bertha feels like she should cry. She is afraid, but also in awe. Half the tree falls down into the yard and yellow flames lick the dry bark and the dead leaves on top. And then there's a sound as though someone is pelting the corrugated-iron roof with pebbles. Balls of ice hit the patch of lawn outside the front door, on the dust. Chickens dash for cover. A downpour of this nature is completely new to her. In two minutes, the landscape has turned to white. Visibility is at a minimum. Wherever Bertha looks, hailstones clatter together and pile up, eventually resembling the scene of an Ohio winter.

The air is washed clean and, through the open window, the smell of wet earth rushes into her nostrils. She loves this, she thinks. This power, this grandeur. The hailstorm ends and rain follows. Nothing like rain in Cleveland: this is a giant bucket of water tipped over the earth from high above, a drenching that carves deep furrowing rivers in the hail and makes ochre pools out of the dips in the terrain.

The downpour quenches the burning tree. Bertha looks at the blackened trunk sliced in half and wonders at it. She thinks of Moses and the burning bush. God did not speak to her from that burning bush and did not tell her to lead her people to a new land. But some voice has been whispering to her all along, that she must trust her destiny and follow it, so that her children and grandchildren can be born on this continent and call the storms and the highveld home for generations.

As soon as the lightning and thunder ease off, Anna comes rushing into the house, struggling and breathing hard.

*–Medem, you see big fire? You okay, medem?*

*–Yeah, everything's fine, Anna. What about the kids? They okay?*

*–Yes, medem. All okay. Las yeh, Joseph, he die from lightning.* Anna draws an imaginary line across her throat with her finger.

*–That's terrible! Who was Joseph?*

*–Baas-boy. Good man. Too dangerous, this lightning. Stay inside. Keep away from tree and tall things. You get …* Here she draws the imaginary knife across her throat again.

Anna is not a small woman, and she has recently gained further weight. Her size mesmerises Bertha, as do her wide eyes filled with fear at the thought of the now-deceased Joseph and the terrible lightning. There are some unique ways to die in Africa, and getting struck by lightning is one of them. It seems to Bertha a horrifyingly pointless end.

✡

The girl I was, the one who carried violin music in her heart, learns from a young age about all the different ways you can die in South Africa. The first lesson goes something like this and could happen to anyone. You are seven. On a morning trip to school, you stop at the shop with your mother to buy a youngberry Liqui-Fruit juice for school. There, you see an old black man, who is drunk, saying rude words to a young white man who is the shopkeeper. A short while later, the shopkeeper pulls out a gun from behind the counter, and shoots the old man dead. You remember only seeing his old boots sticking out from the grey wool blanket that he's covered with when he's dead. This is the first time you see death. You see someone die for their words.

And so you learn that shooting is probably the most common way to die in South Africa.

As a teen, you walk down an alley in Johannesburg to a restaurant with your friends, and you pass a man standing still against the wall of the alley, blood dripping down his face from a stab wound. Again, you could be anyone. You would know, looking at him, that he could soon die. Stabbing, with either an African panga knife or broken glass, is also a fairly common cause of death in South Africa.

If you are really unlucky, you might be the victim of vigilantes. Again, to qualify for this position, you could be anyone. You would simply have to be in the wrong place at the wrong time, although being black would put you at a higher risk, since someone might easily blame you for being on the wrong political side or something. Many African people through the decades die being 'necklaced': doused with petrol, a car tyre shoved around their shoulders, and set alight. Of all the horrors, this is the one that brings the violin girl terrible nightmares. Likewise, if you are black and arrested in the 1960s or '70s or '80s or early '90s even (again, being at the wrong place at the wrong time is the most likely reason for this happening), you might die a violent death in detention. You might be assaulted, beaten until your skin comes off, shocked, genitally mutilated and then finally you might choke to death on a tennis ball.

Later, though, when Nelson Mandela, the first black president, is elected in South Africa in 1992, and the country rids itself of the title 'Racist Republic', there will be an entire generation of armed youths who have been waiting for a revolution that will never come. After a peaceful transition to black majority rule, the poor are still poor and the armed youths are still armed; to be the victim of the most violent crimes in the country you can be any one of the many hues or cultures of the Rainbow Nation. What puts you at risk is living in South Africa every day.

These are the lessons in harm and death you learn about, growing up in South Africa.

But they are not there yet, in 1938. Only their shadows hover. Those kinds of crimes will shortly emerge in civilised Europe courtesy of the

Nazis, who will perfect the art of subhuman behaviour against six million Jews. This will give other warped souls a blueprint for crimes against humanity. South Africa, during apartheid, will model its death camps on the ones run by the Nazis. And afterwards, the land will be so soaked in blood and crime that the echoes will go on resounding loudly right into the twenty-first century.

Bertha's newly awakened fear of death by lightning in 1937 doesn't register at all on the violin girl's list of terrible ways to die in South Africa.

✡

Later, Anna is cooking dinner and Bertha is reading from a Jewish-American cookbook that Gertrude has sent her, wondering whether ingredients such as cranberries even exist on her new continent. At least she knows she can get apples, and as soon as she can, she will instruct Anna on how to make a real American apple pie.

When Phil comes home from the general store in the early evening, the fury of the storm has passed. Bertha runs into her husband's arms and he holds her close for longer than usual.

At night the smell of recent rain and the beginning of the wet season is an intoxicating force. She feels alive. Electric. Phil is in a loving mood, having had a very productive day at work where the earnings were good. And Bertha knows what she wants. Her whole body tingles with potential.

*–I'm sorry I wasn't here to protect you against the lightning, darling,* he says to her, climbing into bed. *You handled it like a star. You're becoming a bushveld girl after all!*

She throws off her nightie. She leans over him and kisses him.

*–Happy birthday, darling,* she says. *I have a present for you …*

✡

The future is a dark glass. If Bertha could know on the night that her son is conceived, her husband's birthday, what lies in her future, and in her son's distant adult future, would she have the strength to wake up the morning after and breathe in the day as though she is immortal, as though nothing ever will rob her of this joy?

✡

Bee and Phil return from the doctor in Johannesburg. She climbs out of the car, her excitement palpable.

*–I have to write Gertrude and Meyer straight away and tell them!*

*–Yes, darling. Then let's go over this afternoon to Dora and Woolf's for tea. They'll never believe it.*

Morning sickness. The heat of summer. Flies and violent storms roll in over the highveld. An ancient and bloodied continent shapes a new soul that grows in a tentative, delicate way.

Aunt Dora and Uncle Woolf are just like grandparents-to-be. The news that Bee is expecting ripples through the family. A long-awaited letter from Gert arrives:

**RELIANCE STEEL CORPORATION**
1170 IVANHOE ROAD
MAIN OFFICES AT CLEVELAND, OHIO

Dear Bertha:
Received your letter last week. I can't understand xxxx the xxxxxxxxxx casual way in which you accept the fact that you are a prospective mother. It isn't like you. I would expect you to get very excited about it and also very shy towards anybody else. Oh, well, never having had a baby I wouldn't know. Certainly hope it has lots of health, wealth and happiness. And please take care of yourself.

And a few weeks down the track, Mildred Braker and Joshua Lourie get married at the synagogue in Berea, Johannesburg. The wedding is a less grand affair than the Frank–Davidow wedding, but then the bride is not an exotic import from America.

Bee has designed and sewn her own pink dress, which makes no secret of her growing bump. It is small, but she is so slender that the change to her flat stomach is noticeable. Her cousin looks lovely in white. Joshua stands stiffly awaiting the arrival of his bride. He seems a complete stranger to her, and barely looks in her direction. He is a broodingly handsome groom, though his treatment of his new wife seems diffident, uninterested even, as they make their way through the throngs of people. Bee's heart aches for poor Mildred and rages against her rib cage for no good reason. Phil wraps his arm protectively round her expanding waistline.

*Mazel tov.* Blessings rain down on the newlyweds, and good wishes and kisses follow. As Bee hugs her cousin, she is overcome by emotion.

–*I hope you'll be very happy*, she whispers.

–*I'll do my best*, her cousin replies.

When she looks up at Joshua, he stares at her as though he's just been shocked out of a trance.

–*Mazel tov, Joshua.*

–*I suppose I should thank you, Bee*, he says, his words clipped, his lips barely moving. *And I suppose I should appreciate your presence here, despite your … condition. But if you want to do me a favour, stay away and let me get on with my life.*

Up until that moment, Bertha has coped with her nausea. But within moments of that encounter, she is bent over double in the ladies' toilets, vomiting until her heaving body produces nothing more at all.

✡

The nausea persists. Bee finds it hard to gain weight. Phil is a devoted husband, but finds the emotional state of his wife exhausting. One moment she is tearful, accusatory and depressed; the next, she is on top of the world. The conversation that always brings her back into balance revolves around bringing Meyer over to South Africa.

One night, before she goes to sleep, she's thinking about her mother. Her heart feels like it's being crushed beneath her ribs, which is perhaps why she has the nightmare: she's back in Ohio and she's a small child, waking in the dark in her room. She hears her mother coughing and choking, so she leaps out of bed and rushes to her parents' room. But when she gets there, her father stands blocking the entrance. *זי איז טויט.* *She's dead*, he says. *Your mother is dead.* Bertha lets out a scream, fights her father to let her pass, and when she gets into their room, her mother is not there. The bed is neatly made, the sheets folded over the blankets, though it is the middle of the night. She looks out of the window, and moonlight falls on a mound of fresh earth. *Your mother is buried*, her father says. *She's dead and buried.* Bertha screams: *No.* She wakes herself up, hearing her own voice bouncing off the walls. Her eyes fly open and Phil is shaking her, his face frightened, hovering over hers in the starlight.

*–Bert, darling, it's a nightmare, it's just a nightmare.*

*–No*, she sobs, her chest heaving. *It isn't. It isn't! It's true. Help me Phil, I can't breathe!*

*October 19*
*I had a terrible dream last nite about my late mother.*

Halloween comes and goes. No one in South Africa knows what that is. Bertha tempers her disappointment, but when Thanksgiving arrives and again her relatives are clueless about the holiday, the biggest and most important one in the American calendar, she is hit by a wave of homesickness that lasts for weeks.

✡

At Phil's prompting, Bee takes up piano with Mrs Kleynhans. Although Bee only has eight good fingers to work with, Mrs Kleynhans says in her thick Afrikaans accent, *You don't need any more fingers than the ones God gave you, Mevrou Davidow. We will make a plan.*

The music goes into her veins. Each note is a healing force. Even as a beginner, she feels she can play for hours. She has to be laughingly pried away from the instrument at the end of each lesson. Based on this, Phil finds an old piano for her, which comes home to their living room. No matter that the low F is so sharp it's almost a G and that the low C doesn't work at all. There are enough keys higher up to do all the practice she needs. And, she reasons, with fewer working fingers, she can do with fewer working keys. She longs to make real music, but even as she masters simple pieces, she knows that nothing transcendent will ever emerge from her hands. Still, a deeper compulsion propels her to continue with lessons and take herself as far as she might go.

✡

Anna, the servant girl, definitely moves more slowly round the house these days. She finds it hard lifting the stainless steel pots onto the stove to heat the water, and often gets Phineas to help her. Her extra weight is what may be causing the problem, Bertha thinks.

It's Christmas Eve. Bertha and Phil have an early dinner by candlelight. Summer is in full force. The night throbs with crickets and frogs. All the windows are wide open and Anna has just finished washing the dishes.

–*To the most beautiful mother-to-be in the world*, Phil says and raises his glass of water. *I will always forgive your bad temper, because the minute you smile, it's like the sun has come out.*

–*Cheers*, Bertha says, grinning, clinking her glass against his. *I'm not that bad, am I?*

–*Oh, you're like the little girl with the curl right in the middle of her forehead ... when she's good, she's very, very good, but when she's bad she's horrid.*

–*Medem!* Anna's voice comes from the kitchen. *Medem!*

–*What is it, Anna?* Phil calls.

–*Medem!*

Bertha pushes her chair back. There is something desperate in the woman's voice.

–*All right, Anna, I'm coming.*

In the kitchen, Anna is standing over the sink, bent almost double. She's clutching her stomach.

–*Are you ill, Anna? What's the matter?*

–*Madokta, madokta, medem, hurry.*

–*Phil*, Bertha calls. *Can you send for a doctor?*

–*What's the matter with her?*

–*I don't know. She's very ill.*

She looks at the woman's face. It's distorted with pain, glossy with sweat.

–*Aish, aish, aish!* Anna cries. Phil is calling the operator.

At that moment Bertha notices the blood on the floor.

And then Anna collapses. Her legs shake. Her body convulses. Bertha is terrified. This is how someone dies. This woman is clearly dying, she thinks. And then, to Bertha's disbelief, amid a gush of blood and mucus, something wet and shiny emerges from beneath

Anna's uniform, and onto the kitchen floor.

*–Oh my Lord! Phil, come in here! Phil, it's a baby! Anna's had a baby boy!*

✡

In the distance, an African church choir sings until just before dawn. Their voices carry over the bushveld. The cowhide drum connects the singers to their roots, to the ancestors who watch over them, while their voices soar into the universe, connecting them with the God of Christianity, whose blessings they seek.

The kitchen is clean. Bertha never imagined that she would be clamping and cutting a newborn baby's cord on her kitchen floor under instruction from Aunt Dora over the phone. Boy, will she have something to tell Gert!

Later, Phil lies in bed next to her.

He doesn't say anything. They are both thinking that what just happened is women's business. She imagines something must have been wrong for Anna to have bled so, to have been in that much pain. Surely childbirth is not supposed to be so terrible. How could no one have even known that Anna was pregnant?

Dawn arrives. Christmas Day, 1938. Roosters crow and cattle complain of full udders in the surrounding farms. Life is a miracle, and Bertha is glad to have witnessed this much of it.

# PART THREE

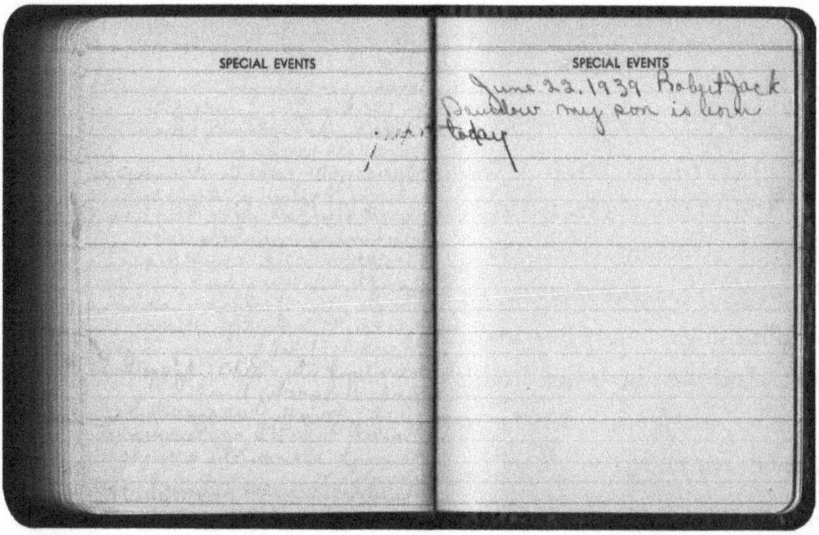


On the winter solstice of 1939, Bertha wrestles her little son into the world. After a long delirium of pain where she hovers on the threshold between life and death, she holds a perfect human being in her arms. Every finger is perfect … every toe. Every hair on his head. Flawlessly made in the image of God. Her flesh. Her blood. Her pain. Her family.

The efficient nurse wants to take him away from her immediately, as is customary, so that he can be weighed, washed, wrapped.

*–He's mine! My son! Don't take him from me, do you understand?* She is shaking. She holds the tiny, slippery body against her own. Under normal circumstances, no hospital staff would take such nonsense from a patient. Perhaps Bertha's American accent floors the nurse. An accent that sounds like a female Franklin D Roosevelt, the American president on the wireless, holds some weight.

The nurse speaks in Afrikaans to her superior, who bustles up to Bertha with a clipboard.

*–Hy kan net vir 'n bietjie by jou bly, mevrou.*

*–I don't understand Afrikaans. Phil! Get my husband in here! Phil!*

–*But ma'am*, says the nurse, who can speak English. *He's got to be washed first!*

–*You get my husband in here, young lady*, says the fierce female version of the American president.

And so she obeys, letting the new father in and rattling away to him in Afrikaans.

–*Dis 'n pragtige seuntjie, meneer!*

Phil nods, barely hearing. All he can think about is that he has a son. And then he is next to his wife, holding a miracle in his arms.

–*We're a family*, Bertha says. *A child and a mother and a father. Please God protect us all.*

✡

As Robert Jack Davidow – Bobby for short – learns to smile, the eyes of the world turn to Europe. Weapons of war are being sharpened and the whispers are that Hitler wants to rule the world. His campaigns of hatred have already begun. Those Jews who have within their blood the throbbing rhythm of fear begin to flee Germany and Poland and other areas where the pogroms still live in their veins. German-speaking Jews trickle into South Africa and the community grows. News spreads about the impending disaster so far away.

✡

At the age of nine, I fall in love with the German language irrevocably after the first term of lessons. Its sounds are a resonant, familiar echo. I love hearing my teacher's voice and imitate the words with accuracy. She is surprised at my ability to make the throaty 'rrr', and the elusive 'ch'. The sentence structure is logical and the complex grammar seems obvious. I love the strength of the words – the essentiality of *gemütlich*, which is somewhere between 'cosy' and 'neighbourly' and 'friendly', and, of course, *Schadenfreude*, which expresses, in a single word, the guilty pleasure someone might experience at someone else's misfortune.

In the tenth year of my life, as spring begins to roll over the highveld, and as I walk through the long grass from the sports field to the classroom, I recite 'Mondnacht' by Joseph von Eichendorff. My soul is stirred by the beauty and romance and stillness of the heavens kissing the earth into silence so that she, the earth, could dream of him. My soul wants to expand like the poet's and fly, like his, through the quiet lands under starlight with outspread wings – home.

While Granny Bee tells me repeatedly that I should not waste my time on this ugly language, I tumble into its warmth and cling to its uprightness. At night as I listen to the noises, the screech of crickets and nightbirds, my traitorous spirit flies through the *Mondnacht* and lodges itself in the cadences of a foreign and abhorred language.

*Es war, als hätt der Himmel*
*Die Erde still geküsst …*

It was as if the heavens
Kissed the earth into silence …

What greater love could there be? I wondered. And the last stanza:

*Und meine Seele spannte*
*Weit ihre Flügel aus,*
*Flog durch die stillen Lande,*
*Als flöge sie nach Haus.*

And my soul spread its wings wide
And flew over the quiet lands
As if it were flying home.

I wanted to be that flier, whatever it took.

✡

Bertha is enclosed in a world of early motherhood. She cannot believe the love she feels for her son, and it strikes her for the first time how terrible it must have been for her own mother, falling ill, knowing she had two little children in the world who needed her. It breaks her when she looks at Bobby.

–*I'm not going to leave you, darling, ever, ever,* she says to him. *I mean to live until you're old, please, God.*

Even though Anna has a little boy of her own now to take care of, she works eight-hour days in the house, with baby Elias tied tightly to her back, his head always turned to the left as Anna brings in steel pots of water, polishes the floor, washes the clothes and the dishes, and sweeps the kitchen. She looks after Bobby too, feeding him, washing him. Sometimes it seems to Bertha that Anna favours Bobby over Elias, spoiling him and talking harshly to Elias when he cries or whimpers.

–*Anna, your son. He's little. Be kind to him, like you are to Bobby.*

–*Aish, medem, no.*

Anna's rationale is that she is protecting him in a brutal society; that the sooner he learns to be tough, the better. He will be a black child in a white man's world, and he should expect no kindness.

The welcoming committee at Uncle Woolf and Aunt Dora's house awaits the arrival of Bertha and Phil and little Bobby. Phil's parents are making the trip, ferried from Johannesburg by Aunt Dora. Bertha cannot wait to show Phil's mother the baby. This is what she's been hoping for all along.

The whole family will be there, for this first outing. Bertha vows if Joshua Lourie shows his face, she will stare right through him.

–*Oy vey!* says the old lady when she arrives, wringing her hands and clutching her husband's sleeve for support. *My grandson, my grandson, let me see him, come here, Bertha, and give him to me!*

The old lady sits down in a waiting chair and Bertha places the red-faced baby in her mother-in-law's arms.

–*Oy, what are you feeding him! He's so heavy! Look at those eyes. Your eyes, Phil's smile, yes, definitely Phil's smile! Now I can die happy, my dear. I've seen what I need to see in this world.*

–*Now let's have none of that talk,* Bertha says, and takes her son back into her arms, kissing the old lady's cheek.

–*Oh Bee, he's just perfect!*

Yetta Mae and Esther crowd in, wanting to hold him, touch him. Uncle Woolf kisses his niece on her head and tickles Bobby under the chin.

–*He looks just like me! Can't wait to give him a taste of sheep's head! Ooh and raw egg, sucked out of the shell while it's still warm. He's certainly his great-uncle's very own nephew!*

–*Uncle Woolf, that's not a very appetising meal for a baby!* Bertha laughs.

–*Ah, but he will love it! It's his culture, his history. Your mother and I loved to eat that when we were kids. I was the one who could get the egg even before it was right out of that chicken's bum …*

–*Woolf!* Aunt Dora cries, frowning in mock fierceness. *Now, let me hold the baby!*

Phil enjoys the status of proud new father. He grins at the onslaught of compliments from his beautiful nieces and his parents. Bertha finds herself irritated: what's he done to deserve all the praise? Did he almost die giving birth? Was his body torn apart, then cut and sewn back together without pain relief? What does he know about getting up every two hours to feed a crying baby until you vomit with exhaustion? About having to put cabbage leaves on infected breasts to take the swelling down and praying that the baby doesn't cry to feed because it's so painful?

Here, there are enough people looking after Bobby. Bertha goes outside. She finds her way out to a small rock that overlooks the veld. There have been fires nearby and patches of burned earth can be seen for miles around. Sometimes the air is so smoky in winter she feels she cannot breathe.

*–Hey, cousin Bee!*

She turns her head.

*–Mildred! How are you, dear?*

*–Oh, I'm so happy to see you! You look wonderful … your cheeks are rosy and you don't look at all fat!* She laughs and skips over to sit on the rock next to her cousin.

*–Who said I was fat?*

*–Who else? Auntie Rose said weeks ago, 'Well, I bet having a baby has taken care of her perfect figure!' She's such a jealous old bat. You look so well. And the baby! He's just the cutest boy in the world.*

*–I adore him.*

*–Oh, I'm envious of you.*

*–Well, don't be. Childbirth – it's not for sissies.*

*–I'm sure there's got to be some pain …*

*–Yeah. If I told you the truth it'd put you off.*

*–I don't imagine it could be worse than …*

*–Worse than what?*

*–You know. Worse than … I can't even say it. Worse than a wedding night?*

*–A wedding night? You mean yours?*

*–Yes. Isn't it something terrible? That pain.*

*–I didn't find it so.*

*–You're so lucky, Bee. I just can't get over it. Every time it's like …* Her voice drops to a whisper. *Honestly, every time the pain is terrible. Every time.*

*–That's awful.* Bee feels hot and distressed and she looks at her cousin's anguished expression.

*–Is Phil a … gentleman?*

*–Yeah, I suppose he is.*

*–Be grateful for him, cousin Bee. He's a good man.*

They are sitting there on the rock when footsteps approach.

*–Speak of the devil,* Mildred whispers, and Bee expects to see Phil.

Both women turn. Joshua Lourie strolls towards them, his hands in his waistcoat pockets, nonchalant, cool.

*–There's a baby crying,* he says. *I think it might be yours.*

Bee gets up quickly, feels the blood rush to her cheeks.

*–Thank you.*

Joshua sits down in her place, next to his wife. Bertha hasn't seen him for months. She's forgotten how tall he is, how dark his hair.

*–Don't mention it. Thank* you.

His eyes catch the light and he looks away from Bee, turning to his wife and sliding his arm around her waist. His fingers spread over her ribs, crushing her to him. Bee catches a glimpse of her cousin's face beneath his, white as the moon in daylight, as his lips come down hard on hers.

✡

Being a baby in Groblersdal has its benefits and its dangers. Bobby gets prize position on Uncle Woolf's lap at Sunday lunch. He watches with admiration when his uncle, as promised, grabs a warm egg right out of a laying chicken and sucks down the yolk. But he turns his head away at the taste that is offered him.

Bee watches her little boy on her uncle's lap with adoring eyes. This is family. This is what it means to be complete. She has travelled so far from the innocent young girl she was when she stepped onto the SS *Berengaria.*

One day Bobby goes limp and hot. And when they finally get him to a hospital Bee is hysterical. He has tick-bite fever. Because his body is so small, it could be too late. It is an eternity until they know whether he will live or die. But his will to live is strong and he defies the odds.

She wants more children. But the risks have already revealed themselves to her.

✡

When Bee finds out she is pregnant again, she is overjoyed, but her elation is short-lived. One evening Phil finds her shivering in bed, her pupils dilated, her eyes wide.

–*The medem, she is no good,* Anna tells Phil urgently as he walks into the house. Phil is horrified at his wife's shaking body and raging temperature. He tells Anna to stay the night in the house to take care of Bobby, and to bring Elias to sleep there too, and he rushes his wife into the car and drives her to hospital.

For a torturous week he watches by her bedside as she battles malaria.

When she finally comes home, pale and rake-thin, she begins to bleed. The new life that would have been falls out of her in a small lump of blood and tissue.

Luckily, Anna carries the burden of the housework and the cooking, and Phineas looks after the gardening and everything else around the house that needs to be done. Phil orders Anna to cook lots of thick South African steaks to give his wife strength again, and hopefully to fatten her up.

Bee eats like a starved lioness. To keep herself from sadness, she immerses herself in being a mother to an energetic toddler.

✡

In Europe, there are rumours of extermination camps for Jews, as Hitler corrupts the continent and stains the earth with the blood of thousands of innocent people.

Bee sits with Phil in the living room after Bobby has gone to sleep. Tonight, more than ever, she longs for the people back home. The veld, the sounds of the African singing, the smell of new rain on dry earth – all of it feels inescapably foreign. She is reading a letter from her dear brother. Meyer is very sorry about her miscarriage, and is certain it was just a stroke of very bad fortune that she contracted malaria while pregnant. She opens a letter from Gertrude, who also sends her sympathies.

> Dear Bertha,
>
> I received your last letter with the adorable pictures June 15, which was exactly 32 days from the day you wrote it. That isn't bad for war time. I was very shocked to learn about having malaria fever and am glad you are recovered. Will it have any after effects? I thought you had enough vaccinations to prevent everything. Also, about Bobbie, I just read an article in the Reader's Digest about a cure for tick fever, if he should get it, but I hope he is also all right now. Gosh, you sure have lived in the last few months. Leon and I felt very badly about it all, and especially about losing your child. Please try and take care of yourself, and I hope it won't be too long

before you can try again to increase your family, and also, thank God for Bobbie. There are so many people who can't even get the first one.

Leon Weiner is Gerty's new husband. Al signed up for medical school at Ohio State, and is busy with some pre-med courses. Bee wonders whether Gert married for love's sake or for financial security. She can imagine her friend ultimately making a pragmatic rather than a romantic choice. She wonders, briefly, what kind of a choice she herself made.

Lately, when she receives letters from Gert, she can no longer relate so easily to the priorities that used to be hers. Things sure have changed.

She sinks into memories of Jack Girick and Michael Sharlitt; she sees images of the Jewish Orphan Home and the trees growing bigger over the walkway she once trod with Gertrude. It's been a long while since she heard from Arleen. She received one letter after Bobby's birth, which revealed how hard life was for Arleen as she took care of ailing older relatives.

*–Why so quiet, darling?*

*–I'm thinking of home.*

*–This is home now, isn't it?*

*–Of course.*

*–You still upset about the baby?*

Silence.

*–I can give you another one, you know.*

Nine months later Bee goes into labour. This birth is both an assault and a blessing. She wants to die, the pain is so unbearable, but in the breaths between contractions she knows that there is nowhere else she'd rather be than having this baby.

In four hours, she gives birth to an angel. A little girl with pink fists and almond-shaped eyes. Her heart fills to bursting as she holds her tiny daughter in her arms.

–*My darling*, she says, and kisses the soft head.

Phil comes in that evening and brings Bobby to see his new sister. Bee holds her two children as close as she can, and Phil, not one easily given to emotion, lets tears run down his cheeks.

–*I miss my mom*, Bee says. *I wish she were here.*

As is the custom, the nurses come to take the baby away for the night. Phil and Bobby go home and Bee does all she can to prolong the time she can have with her daughter.

–*You need your sleep*, the nurse insists, and takes the baby off Bee's breast. The baby screams and Bee begins to cry, but she doesn't have any strength in her to ask for her child back.

In the morning, after very little sleep because her breasts are hurting like hell, she asks for her daughter immediately.

–*I'm afraid we've had to put her in a special care unit*, the nurse says.

–*What?*

–*It's not too bad. She's got a bit of jaundice and we just need to monitor her.*

–*Jaundice? Is that serious?*

–*It's very common, Mrs Davidow. She'll be all right. Just have your breakfast now and you can come and see her in a little bit.*

The child in the plastic bubble is yellow. Hours go by like centuries. Voices fade in and out. She thinks they keep telling her to eat. Her breasts leak milk down her gown and she doesn't care. Any modesty is gone. She watches the child go from yellow to orange. She thinks the nurses help her out of the ward and back to her hospital bed. She imagines she is dying. No, it's her mother dying. She can't be sure if she's dreaming. The night is a stormy sea of milk and blood.

In the morning, a nurse is sitting on the end of her bed. Her face is pale. Bee doesn't register the words at first.

*–I'm deeply sorry to inform you, Mrs Davidow, that baby Davidow passed away in the night.*

The scream that comes from her mouth is not made by her but pulled from her. Perhaps a doctor comes in. Perhaps someone administers an injection. Everything beyond her scream is dark and out of time.

And when she remembers who she is, she's at home, in bed, and Phil is stroking her hand, while Anna cajoles Bobby to eat his lunch in the kitchen. Was it all a nightmare?

*–Phil, where's the baby?* she says, feeling her full milky breasts, the pad between her legs, the pain of a recent tear. Her voice is weak, like an old woman's.

He shakes his head. His shoulders move and she sees him sobbing, holding his head in his hands. So she turns her face to the pillow and faints.

*They let her die*, she says in her dream. *That stinking, God-forsaken African hospital. They killed my daughter, my beautiful whole little girl. They took her from me and put her in a plastic cot and she died because I wasn't there to love her, to hold her and protect her against the world. She thought she had been abandoned, so she died. I didn't abandon you!* She tries to scream in her dream but her voice is blocked. *I love you! You should have been born in America. I should never ever have come to Africa. Never never never never …*

If it were not for Bobby, she would loosen her hold on life. The bottomless hole in her soul can never be fixed.

The baby's funeral is on a Sunday.

At four in the afternoon, a car door slams. Boots crunch across the gravel. Phil isn't meant to be home for another hour. There's a loud knock on the door and the sound of voices. Then Anna comes cautiously into her room.

*–Medem, is Boss Joshua, to come see you.*

Bee says nothing. She pushes the covers off the bed, swings her legs over the side and shrugs on a pink dressing-gown. Beneath the fabric, milk sticks to her breasts like old tears. She sits down at her dressing table and runs a comb through wavy hair. Her face is unrecognisable to her.

She enters the living room. Joshua Lourie is silhouetted in the doorframe with the afternoon sunlight behind him. When he steps into the house, she sees that behind him, on the porch, is a small coffin. Its lid is ajar.

Somewhere in her vague memory of the last few days, Phil's words, which she knows she must have heard, live on: *Joshua Lourie will make the coffin.*

Bee looks at Joshua, broken. He opens his arms and she walks into a space that has been waiting for her.

She doesn't know how long they stand there in the silence of the dead afternoon. She can feel the rough material of his suit under her hands, his chin resting on her head, his arms wrapped around her.

Her heart aches against his. It will never be whole again. She knows only one thing: a love which creates itself despite every attempt to destroy it cannot be undone. There are no words for this kind of grief, or this kind of love.

✡

After the baby's death, as World War II suffocates the whole of Europe, Bee receives news from Meyer: he's been called up to join the army. He will be leaving for France, where his typing skills will come in handy in the effort against the Germans. Bee is not to worry, he says: he won't be out on the frontline. Oh, and he's changed his name to Mike, because that's what most of his friends call him now.

Bee thinks her heart might not hold out in this world.

Under these crisp southern skies, it is impossible to imagine the freezing terror sweeping across Europe. The sound of Hitler's voice on the radio is an indicator of the darkest possibilities of the human soul. Because of the Yiddish words buried in the recesses of her memory, Bee can decode Hitler's ranting fury against her people.

✡

Many decades later, the girl who used to play the violin sits on the verandah listening to the music of rain falling on the tin roof, on the slasto paving, on the muddy earth.

–*One day I'm going to leave South Africa and go to Germany to learn German*, she says, feeling like a rebel. Granny Bee, visiting that Sunday, cannot support such an idea, even if only in theory.

–*I am getting all A's in German*, the girl continues.

–*But darling, why Germany?*

–*I dunno.*

–*It's an ugly place where terrible things happened. And with an ugly language. You're too young to understand but that language reminds me of the Nazis and all the suffering of our relatives.*

–*But Gran, didn't your dad and mom speak Yiddish?*

–*Of course, darling!*

*–And isn't Yiddish just like German?*

*–I believe they are spoken differently.*

The former violin-player holds her tongue. She doesn't want to cause distress, and the full meaning of Granny Bee's unhappiness eludes her. Neither does she fully understand the depth of her compulsion to go one day and immerse herself in this foreign place.

But one thing is for certain: her love for German has been compounded by a German boy who has arrived in class and captivated her attention.

✡

The memory of the lost baby hovers over Bee. She has little energy to think of things outside the house. Phil and Woolf are busy, and she assumes business is going well, but her thoughts are on making a home and ensuring that Bobby stays healthy and happy.

The influx of Jewish immigrants from Europe increases. When the Davidows go to shul in Johannesburg, they notice the congregation has more than doubled in a few short months.

Soldiers getting ready to be deployed visit the general store. Sometimes Bee helps out in the afternoons and enchants the young men with her smile. It's a comfort for them to talk to her, to see her with her little son, doing the normal everyday things that mothers do.

Bee has been collecting books and now has a substantial library, which she shares with anyone who is interested. Everyone, except some of her closest relatives, see her as the star, the beautiful American with the home full of books. No one who meets Bee at this time would guess at the valleys and chasms beneath her composed exterior.

South Africa is divided into groups of different races and languages. Bee learns that the old antagonism between the British and the Boers has largely faded. But members of the far-right-wing Afrikaans community have recently made public their affinity with Hitler's sentiments. Blacks and Jews, they agree, should be eliminated.

These people are members of the Ossewabrandwag, a pro-Nazi movement led by a Meneer Van Rensburg; once a fortnight, they come into Groblersdal to their meeting in the hotel adjacent to the general store.

Bobby, with his baby American accent, toddles down the street holding hands with his mother and hears a man shouting in the hotel.

*–Death to the Jews! Death to the Jews! Death to kaffirs and Jews!*

He doesn't understand the words, but by his mother's frown and pallor, he can tell things are not good. He clings to her legs and wants her to pick him up.

*–Darling, you're too heavy for me now. Come on, let's walk quickly together back to Daddy's shop.*

And after the meeting in the hotel, leading members of the Ossewabrandwag saunter casually into the general store and buy drinks and snacks, joking with Woolf and Phil, and smiling indulgently at the beautiful startled face of Phil's American wife, who arrives at the entrance to the store and freezes when she sees who the customers are.

As a white person, Bee is a privileged citizen. As a Jew, however, she is afraid of these loud men with their confusing and terrifying rhetoric. They must be simply clueless about the heritage of the Davidows and the Brakers.

News arrives in Groblersdal that the *Dunbar Castle* has been hit by German mines off the coast of West Africa on its journey from

Europe to Beira in Mozambique. The kind captain, the very same man who was so gracious to Bee on her way to South Africa, the one whose eyes twinkled when she saw him again on her honeymoon in Lourenço Marques, is dead.

Bee tries to imagine the thirty minutes that it took for the entire steamship to sink to the cold Atlantic Ocean floor. For a while, she wakes up gasping for breath at night as currents drag her into the bottomless deep.

✡

The war in Europe echoes in the lives of Jews everywhere.

–*My second cousins are dead*, Phil says one night as they sit in the living room after dinner. *They were taken to a concentration camp, Buchenwald. I never knew them, but it makes me sick. A whole family. The mother, the father, the two boys.*

Bee stops reading a letter from Gert and looks up at Phil's face. She loves him, there is no doubt of that. But perhaps she is damaged. She wonders whether something died in her with her daughter. Or perhaps things have always been this way. At any rate, something has changed. She doesn't know if she feels at all how a wife should feel about her husband.

–*It's awful, darling*, she says. *I don't want to think about it. I wish Meyer, Mike, could leave France.*

Those who can escape Hitler move outward in every direction. Others, fortunate enough to be far away already, feel the crimes committed against their own kind as an unbearable burden. Surely this must end!

The sound of the German language is the sound of the obliteration of an entire people. But behind the words spoken by Bee's German-Jewish friends, there lies a narrative of loss that reminds her of her parents: of Jacob and the pogroms that he managed to escape when he left Vilnius so long ago, and of Ethel and her lost battle to live and be a mother in her new country.

✡

When I am fifteen I fall in love with my German boy. I have known him a few years, but overnight he has turned into a cross between Mr Universe and God. We're both on the school's volleyball team and swimming team, and in the blazing afternoons we trudge down to the sports field together, our black swimsuits under our blue and white sports uniforms, our eyes squinting against the brightness. The school has a huge field, two tennis courts and a glittering pool. We are used to having infinite space and walking a long way to get from one activity to the next.

In early September, the water is still freezing, but Mrs Du Plessis, otherwise known as Doopie, or Mrs Two-Plus-Three, has no time for weaklings or chickens, as she calls those of us who baulk at the cold water. *It's good for you*, she tells us. The smell of chlorine will forever be a reminder of Tuesdays – sports day.

We take off our uniforms by the side of the pool, boys at the deep end, girls at the shallow end. As we line up for a relay, I stare at his perfect and very adult body, and I know that I will do anything under God's own heaven to be near him. On the count of three, I plunge into the water, and though the cold knocks all the breath out of me, I swim for my life so that our team gets a head start. Later, as we're towelling ourselves dry, he walks past the line of girls who, like me, can't deny his stunning presence and says:

–*Good swimming, Noddy!*

Noddy is a term of endearment, of course. But reserved for buddies. You don't call the girl of your dreams Noddy.

Doopie walks by and yells at us.

*–Get a move on, you lot. If you want to waste time you can pick up stones for the next hour.*

Punishment for wicked time-wasters is to sit in the sun and fry, whilst picking stones and weeds from the grass. It's a pointless and never-ending task, and no one wants to do it, but as she turns her back, and because he is looking at me, I flare my nostrils and pull a monster face at her. He laughs, leans closer to me, punches me in the arm and says:

*–Shell, you're such a hose!* This, I suppose, is a compliment.

In the months that follow, he swells in my world to gigantic proportions. He becomes the whole of Von Eichendorff's heaven, and I turn into the waiting earth, knowing that I will live in anguish for the rest of my life if he does not kiss me.

The only way to get near him is to live inside his language until it becomes my own. This is why I decide, in the winter of that same year, to leave South Africa for Germany.

I am going to the north, so that I can learn High German. I will stay in Braunschweig with a family I know only briefly, from a time when the husband and wife taught at my school. My passage to Germany is secured on the basis of a single conversation with the wife, in which I express that I would love to go to Germany one day, and in which she offers exuberantly to host me, should I ever come across.

✡

Thanksgiving, 1944: Bee still misses Gert and Al and Arleen and Meyer, but the baby has displaced every other loss. Phil and Bobby are her world. Letters from home and old friends remind her how life in another hemisphere goes on. They connect her to the past and to who she once was. She still hasn't heard back from Al, who is stationed, she thinks, somewhere in Italy. Her letter to him left South Africa in May; she hopes he is alive. She thinks back on their childhood, and his hopeless crush on her. She wishes she had been more generous to him, more understanding, but she's not sure what that would have meant.

Bobby begins school. His English is American, and he speaks fluent Afrikaans without an accent. He also speaks Zulu. In the afternoons he plays with the native children and white children alike under the naked highveld skies. His mother suffocates him with her constant concern about his well-being.

✡

I arrive in Germany in the middle of a sticky European summer. The damp air and long pale days are foreign and cloying. The beautiful *Fachwerk* house that I come to live in looks exactly like my quintessential idea of Germany. The attic at the top is my room. It has slanting windows in the roof and I can see the sky. The house smells of hazelnuts and chocolate and pine. The garden, like many others in the neighbourhood, is meticulously kept. The Strassenbahn is a ten-minute walk away and goes directly to my new school.

Everywhere, there is the sound of German, and the sight of German words. I smile excitedly at my new society, trying to catch the eyes of strangers, wanting to welcome every German human being into my heart. I'm surprised that I'm met with stony stares. On my first attempt to ride the Strassenbahn, a large man shoves me out of the way to get ahead of me.

After two days I feel such homesickness for Africa, and for my friends and family, that it makes me ill.

I am as friendly and open as I am at home, but often, as I'm eating, or when I speak, the *Mutter* of the family reprimands me:

–*Nein! Das tut Man nicht. Das sagt Man nicht. Das ist doof.* It's not the done thing … it's not the said thing. It's stupid.

I try to help around the house as much as possible. Eventually the family sits back and expects that I will do the dinner dishes, and then the lunch dishes as well, when I come home from school.

After some weeks the mother of the family tells me:

–*Your parents are not paying enough to support you. You will have to work properly for your keep.*

I say, *We can just let them know and they'll send enough.*

–*You still have to work for your keep.*

This means that on Sundays, which is the only free day because I have school six days a week, the floors must be scrubbed. After they are scrubbed, they must be inspected by *Mutter*, who will tilt her head just so, to look for any spots that have not been cleaned properly, revealed by the summer light streaming through the window. It usually takes most of Sunday to get the floors just right.

My parents send extra money, but my job is still essential. I retreat into quiet, hardly saying a word in English or German. I want to go home but I don't even speak the language half-fluently yet, and I have never seen snow. I don't want to fail myself. It would be a betrayal of my goal, of my desire to reach the heart of my German boy. So I find ways to survive. I read my German poets and listen to German pop music. The husky voice of Nena singing *Neunundneunzig Luftballons* pulses through my Walkman. The language is still warm in me but now there is an opposing emotion when I hear the words coming from *Mutter*'s mouth. She wants me to eat a hot lunch at school, which she will pay for, but for which I must work harder.

–*In Deutschland essen wir immer warmes Mittagessen.*

Even if everyone always eats a hot lunch in Germany, I decline it – politely. So *Mutter* sits down and tells me in German how much she hates me.

*–Ich hasse dich, verstehst du? Soll ich es auf Englisch erklären, damit es ganz Klar ist?*

*–Wirklich nicht nötig. Ich verstehe alles, danke.*

I try to be polite. I learn the skills of imaginary wall-building, sometimes brick by brick, and so I mostly keep crazy *Mutter* outside my soul.

*Vater* is much kinder. Sometimes, if *Mutter* is upstairs with their young son, he helps me with the dinner dishes. The kinder he is to me, however, the more furious *Mutter* becomes, until being in the house is unbearable.

One night, after all the plates have been dried, he takes me in his arms and tells me in English that I am a very nice girl. That he loves me. At first I think he's being kind, to make up for his mad wife's behaviour. But the way he holds me is too tight, too long, and I panic, shove him away from me and run upstairs.

*Mutter*'s birthday comes and *Vater* gives her a card. On the front of the card is a picture of a man and woman looking at each other. The words are the man's and he's saying:

*... Wir sollen mehr ... (we should)*

And inside the card there's a picture of the two characters in bed, obviously naked, and the text continues:

*... Unterhalten ... (talk more)*

*Mutter* laughs hysterically and I pretend to have understood nothing, but I excuse myself and leave the table.

I do not see until three decades later that a Jewish girl was scrubbing floors for an unhappy, vindictive German woman, and that Braunschweig, Germany, is just over a thousand kilometres from the beginning of my great-grandfather Jacob's journey.

In December, Bee receives what she has been waiting for. The envelope is stained and the ink is smudged, as though it has been rained on. She would know this handwriting anywhere. It has changed and evened out since childhood, but there is no mistaking that a letter from Al has finally arrived. Her mouth dries up for no good reason. Perhaps she is simply relieved that he is still alive.

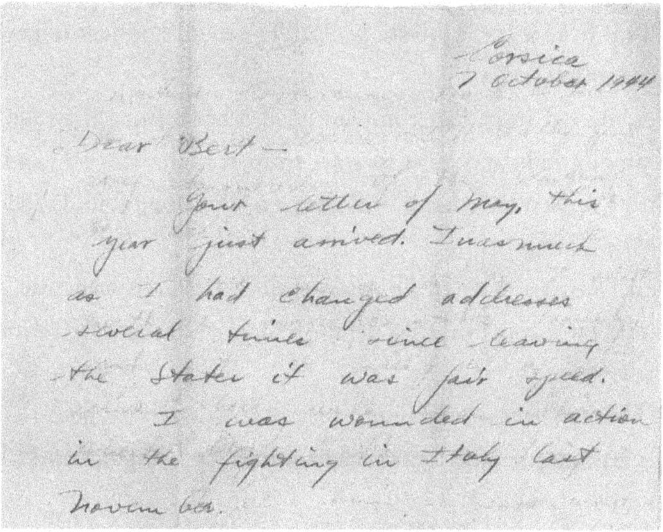

Corsica
7 October 1944

Dear Bert –

Your letter of May, this year just arrived. Inasmuch as I had changed addresses several times since leaving the States it was fair speed.

I was wounded in action in the fighting in Italy last November.

Corsica
7 October 1944

Dear Bert –

Your letter of May this year just arrived. Inasmuch as I had changed addresses several times since leaving the States it was fair speed.

I was wounded in action in the fighting in Italy last November.

Bee looks around at the room. She suddenly feels panicky. Al, wounded in action. She wants to cry.

> My injury prevents me going back to the eternal mud-slinging, dogged fighting lines. But I do carry on in a more or less administrative capacity now …
>
> Once in a while I visit with a very hospitable family and get to sleep in a genuine bed – with clean white sheets. Boy! That's something. I've been 3 years now, drafted from pre-med school. Made the jump from a buck private to 2nd lieutenant and just today got my promotion to 1st LT.
>
> Yes, Bert, I intend to complete med school. But I'll be an old man among kids and have to start from scratch. The war and all the hell I've seen have left a void where a fairly solid foundation for medicine used to be.
>
> Mike hasn't written in a long, long time. I've been very busy. Am currently on a court-martial detail, besides running a detachment of men.
>
> If you can't see … the continuity of this letter, it's because the rain is leaking thru the tent – the candles keep going out and I lose my train of thought.
>
> I have been overseas about 14 months and am thoroughly and pleasantly convinced that there is no place like America. Absolutely not!

The letter trembles in Bee's hands. She looks out at the purple blossoms of a jacaranda tree in full bloom against a quiet twilight sky. She tries to imagine how the young boy in Ohio has become a first lieutenant in charge of soldiers in a terrible war, halfway across the world. And here she is, far from the trenches, from the horrors being committed against her people. She wills him to survive, to outlive his enemies. His words swim in front of her eyes as she looks down.

> I'm really happy to know your little son is coming along so grand.
>
> The war has been long and I expect will be much longer. (I hope to high heaven I'm wrong.) But I've fought the Germans and they are professional soldiers, and that makes a difference.
>
> I expect to be away at least another two years. Then, if I don't get sent to the Pacific, I'll be able to start again and study something constructive, instead of destructive ...
>
> I must make an inspection of my men on guard, so I'll leave you Bert, knowing I enjoyed hearing from you. And may you and yours be in the pink of health. Smile, always,
>
> Your pal, Al.

When Phil comes home, he finds her folding the letter and sliding it back into the envelope.

*–Is everything all right, darling?*

She nods.

*–Have you been crying?*

She shakes her head. *I was hoping to get a letter from Meyer, that's all. I'm worried about him, with what's going on in France right now.*

✡

Despite Al's predictions, the Germans are being hounded into retreat by May 1945. Pictures are emerging of prisoners who have survived the Holocaust and the images are unbearable to see. Bee's concern is for Mike, still stationed in France and still in an administrative position, and for Al, though it looks indeed like the war might soon be over: Goebbels and his wife have killed their children and committed suicide. There are people in the world who do not deserve to be members of the human race, Bee thinks. She sends a picture to her beloved brother to let him know she is all right.

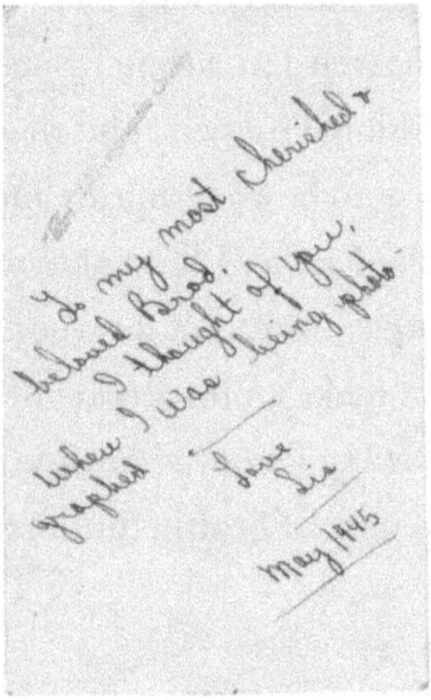



✡

My time in the house with crazy *Mutter* ends unexpectedly. A pair of twins in my class tell their mother at home that there is a girl from South Africa in school, *ein Mädchen, das immer weint.* So the girl who always cries finally meets the twins' mother; the word *Mutter* in this context is suddenly strong and full and dependable. She asks me:

–*Shelley, bist du glücklich?*

I shake my head and say no, I'm not happy at all. And words begin to spill out: about the floors and the angry, crazy *Mutter*, and how I want to stay in Germany and how my work is never good enough. I don't say anything about the *Vater* with his too-soft voice and his hugs and confessions of love.

–*Genau wie Aschenputtel*, she says, and for the first time I smile and I agree, yes, exactly like Cinderella.

And this is how I come to stay with my real German *Mutter. Vater* is a former university chancellor. They ask me if I would like to live with them. I am so thankful that both of them know what it means to love a child as a child, and not as a slave or a surrogate wife. They go together to pack all my things at the *Aschenputtel* house. I don't even have to ever return to see crazy *Mutter* again.

In my new family, the twins' little sister is adopted from India, and she and I bond while we are playing *Pferdereiten* on the floor. I am the horse, and she is the rider, and I gallop across the basement on my hands and knees, acquiring spectacular carpet burn while she shrieks with joy and sits on my back, her long black pigtails whipping against her cheeks.

One day at dinnertime, real *Mutter* says:

–*Woher hast du deine Mandelaugen?*

I tell my new family that my heritage is Lithuanian; I tell them about Jacob David Frank, and his escape from the pogroms. I say that my Jewish background is probably the reason for my brown-black almond eyes. And after a short silence, *Vater* says he thought so, and tells me he wants to show me something.

In his basement, the shelves are littered with books. One entire section is devoted to the Holocaust. *Vater* tells me it must never be forgotten, lest it happen again. He speaks to me in beautiful High German, using his extensive academic vocabulary. I nod and strain to understand, catching as much of it as I can. And then he tells me that he was once part of the Hitler Youth. These books are his way of confronting the realities he did not grasp in his young ignorance. He has seared onto his brain every anguished image of the suffering in Jewish concentration camps. He invites me to look, to read, but I tell him I can't. Everything is already in my blood. Nothing that is written can tell me anything that I don't already know under my skin.

This is his atonement. I am his atonement.

No longer do I have to work for my keep. Instead, I am given the grand cultural tour of northern Germany. On a grey day, when all the trees have lost their leaves and the grass has died, we visit the Wall, the division between East and West Germany built after the war, and wave at the poor guard employed to shoot anyone who dares to try crossing to the other side. I visit an important politician who lives in a medieval stone castle on the Rhine, and I observe the intricate production process of a porcelain factory – things a child from a struggling family in Africa might never expect to experience.

Winter descends. The light fades by three in the afternoon. My skin goes so white I can see my veins pulsing blue at my temples and on my wrists. I never understood why we were called 'whites' in South Africa. I thought our skin colour was closer to gold, but now I see how pale I am. The colour qualifies me as one of South Africa's privileged citizens: I don't have to go home to a violent township at night; I don't need to riot and chant and pray for a revolution just so that I can vote and be treated with common human decency. And yet here, in this land, just forty years before, my *Mandel* eyes and my blood would have put me in death's insistent shadow.

December is so cold that I cannot imagine how humans first decided to live in such a hostile climate. It's minus ten degrees Celsius when we go into Braunschweig to listen to a recital. The streets are aglow with Christmas lights in every shop window. We have come to hear some of Handel's great works, including selections from the *Messiah*, played by the the visiting Berlin Philharmonic Orchestra. The German-Jew-turned-English-Christian wrote his *Messiah* in one continuous outpouring, and when he was finished he wept and said that he had been touched by God.

The first piece that the orchestra plays is the *Largo*. I do not know then that this was Granny Bee's graduation piece. I will only discover this in a letter that I open almost thirty years into the future. So I think I am just soft, and sad because I gave up the violin. The music stirs me so much that *Mutter* scrambles in her bag to find me a tissue because my nose is running and tears have made smudges down the side of my face.

✡

May 9, 1945. Victory Day. The news emerges in South Africa that Adolf Hitler, his wife and Heinrich Himmler have all committed suicide.

But the Afrikaners in Groblersdal are still convinced that the Nazis were correct in identifying Jews and blacks as the scourge of humanity. Even as the world is just beginning to feel the scope of the Nazis' atrocities, Afrikaans nationalists in South Africa are plotting a caste system that will come into being when they come to power in 1948: apartheid.

Bee dislikes the throaty sounds of Afrikaans. It reminds her of the absence of kindness. But Bobby is at home in all the languages around him, with enough Zulu and Sotho to be able to get by with his friends. Sometimes he forgets which language he is speaking. To Bee, these foreign tongues are constant reminders that she is not at home.

✡

Christmas, 1984: my German family and I take a trip.

To Buchenwald.

We get out of the car on Christmas Eve and walk into a forest.

*–Hast du schon mal vom Buchenwald gehört?*

*Vater* asks me this question and he's a little tentative. I nod, Granny Bee's stories in my mind.

Thin tall trees grow like pencil lines to the sky. The air is white. The ground is the colour of ash. The scene looks like a black-and-white film, and as the wind whispers through the dead branches, they are still here: the prisoners crucified upside down, hung from the trees with their arms tied behind their backs. The name given to this forest: the Screaming Wood, because of their cries. As far as the eye can see – a landscape of death by hard labour. They are still here, the imprints of the skeletal bodies of the 55,000 human beings who died here. A cry is under my skin and I can't walk anymore. Suddenly I can hear how German could be an ugly language.

*–Shelley, bist du OK?*

*–Ich würde gerne nach Hause gehen. Mir geht's nicht so gut.*

And when we get home I come down with a fever and I can hardly move for a week.

*Why do you want to go there, darling?* Granny Bee's words resound in my head and she tells me again about the dead cousins and the many family members – cousins, nephews, nieces, aunts, uncles, on both her and Grandpa Phil's sides – who vanished from the world and left nothing but their fear in our veins.

And in my fever I try to answer her, to explain the language, its beauty and its strength, the part of it that is us, that is me, mine, and my love for the German boy. And I try to tell her how I now understand the ugliness, the shadows, and how I am blindly part of something larger than me that wants to heal, only I don't know what it is.

And when I recover, I go down into *Vater*'s study and take out some of the books on Buchenwald and read about its liberation from the Germans by Allied forces on April 11, 1945, twenty-four years – to the day – before I was born.

For weeks, I have very little to say. After speaking only German for months, my jaw is tired of making guttural sounds in the back of my throat; my muscles are exhausted from trying to wrap my tongue, perfectly and without error, around these foreign words.

–*Wieso sagst du so wenig?* my little Indian sister asks me.

–*Ich bin müde.*

One day it snows. I wake up on a dark school morning and my Indian sister is hopping from foot to foot in the kitchen.

–*Es hat geschneit! Es hat geschneit!* she says. Her eyes are black coals exploding with excitement. She knows how I've been wishing for snow.

So, she and I rush out into the morning after clambering into boots and coats. I turn my face to the sky. Never-before-seen snowflakes fall onto my nose, onto my tongue. I take out my hand from its sweaty glove: intricate hexagons made by the universe live for a second on my palm, just long enough for me to wonder at their beauty.

Before the sun comes up I learn how to lie on my back and make snow angels. We build a snowman together and my nine-year-old sister is delighted that a fifteen-year-old can be so childish and so easily pleased by making a carrot nose and stone eyes.

✡

I spend my last winter months in Germany embracing the cold, learning to ski in Switzerland, and swearing in a cavalier fashion *ohne Akzent*, which earns me good buddies amongst the boys. I love the use of *Scheisse* for every object of teenage derision. I treasure the way the German language allows for compound nouns: a *Scheisskerl*, or a *Scheisskopf* or *Scheissarbeit* or having a *Scheissmutter* are images worthy of worship. An awful guy is not just a shit guy, but a Shitguy; awful work is Shitwork; to have homework is to have Shithomework.

When I really don't care either way *es ist mir Scheissegal* – literally, 'it's shit-the-same', which sounds so much better than 'I don't give a shit'.

I am in the middle of a swearing extravaganza one day with some boys outside class when Herr Gruber, the social-studies teacher, walks by and takes note of my colourful conversation. His stern stare stops me in my tracks.

–*Sie sind richting in der Sprache 'rein*, he comments. I'm bursting with relief that he isn't furious. Anyway, *es ist mir Scheissegal* whether he approves or not.

I am, as he's noticed, right in the language, swimming in it as though I have come home.

When I leave Germany, my Indian sister writes me a farewell, which I open on the plane:

> *Liebe Shelley, Du warst einmal bei mir im Winter. Da haben wir einen Schneemann gebaut.*

> Dear Shelley, You were once with me in winter. There, we built a snowman.

✡

I arrive back in South Africa at the peak of summer. January is the month of crackling afternoon thunderstorms and baking earth.

When I walk into the airport building, people look as though they are standing in golden light. The colour of their faces, their skin, is radiant amber. Which must mean that I am white. My friends and family rush to welcome me home, but I only have eyes for my German boy, who takes me into his arms.

–*Welcome home, Noddy! Let's hear your German.*

*–Was soll ich denn sagen?*

He collapses in a fit of giggles and holds me away from him, shaking me like I must be under a spell which he can loosen.

*–That's so scary, man. You sound just like a bloody German!*

I've returned into the year I will turn sixteen. The year I realise that I love my German boy so much, that being *Aschenputtel* and going through the darkness at Buchenwald were all necessary steps on the long winding journey towards my first kiss.

✡

I never tell Granny Bee about the visit to Buchenwald. I tell her about how I read in *Vater*'s basement that the Ashkenazi Jews can be traced back to a group of German women who lived in the Rhine Valley in the Middle Ages. The Yiddish that was carried to Eastern Europe and that came with Jacob to America is *our* Yiddish. Old German is ours as much as it is theirs. We are each other, Germans and Ashkenazi Jews, bound through blood and language.

She doesn't believe me.

But even for Granny Bee, my German comes in useful. On one of my Sunday-afternoon visits to her flat, she introduces me to her friend Lettie, who is older than Bee and who survived the war. Also, she is very, very rich.

*–Speak German to her, darling. She was held by the Germans in a camp for two years, you know.*

I perform like a well-trained circus animal and jump through all the hoops she sets. I use the polite *Sie* and never *Du* for 'you'. At first I am only intent on pleasing my grandmother and showing her that perhaps going to Germany was not in vain. If she can use me as an entertainment piece and I can win points for her from her rich friends, my trip to the land of the enemy might not be such a blight on my record. *Such a good girl, your granddaughter,* Lettie might say. *Here, I'll leave you half of all my fortune in my will.* That, of course, will never happen – I know that, and Bee knows that, as I converse politely with our Holocaust survivor.

Soon, the superficial thoughts fade. Lettie asks me about Germany and I suddenly want to tell her about my visit to Buchenwald. In German. She is quiet for some time after I finish. She compliments me on my flawless High German and Granny Bee glows with pride. I am afraid to ask Lettie what horror she lived through. But she tells me. In German-inflected English:

*–I saw my father shot in front of me at Dachau. I saw my mother and sister herded to the gas chamber. I saw the magnitude of evil that humankind is capable of. I will never forget.*

*–Lettie, tell Shelley about your blue eyes and how that saved you.*

*–Meine Augen. Ja, meine Rettung. I survived because of a betrayal. An SS man. I reminded him of his teenage daughter. I was the only one with blue eyes in the family. Saved by him. Sent under cover of darkness out of the camp to a German family with four blue-eyed children. They later put me on a boat that was taking refugees to England because they were afraid for their own lives.*

*–Tell her about Frank, Lettie. And the SS man.*

*–Ja, okay. On the boat I met my husband, Frank. We came on a cargo ship to South Africa soon after. But I heard the SS man was killed. Shot in the head by his own comrades. They discovered his betrayal. So his children lost him because he had a softness in his heart for another child.*

*–Ich finde es schwierig zu verstehen. Wie schaft Man alles nachher?* I ask. I don't understand how one manages afterwards.

*–The most powerful emotion is forgiveness. Hatred is of no use. I bear no malice towards any human being. I will never forget, but I have forgiven.*

It is only later that I will learn how as we speak then, Lettie and Bee and I, the South African government forces are committing crimes against humanity of the same nature, in the name of white supremacy. There will be a time near the turn of the century, after the horror, after the damage, when victims will face their torturers, or the murderers of their children, look them in the eye during the Truth and Reconciliation Commission of the 1990s, and say *I forgive you for the terrible harm you have done.*

Meeting Lettie is the first time I encounter an unfathomable capacity in human beings: the ability to forgive those whose hearts are the darkest.

✡

A world war has been and gone. Europe lies in ashes.

But for Bee, the world is brightening again. Her precious brother Meyer, aka Mike, has written her the letter she's been waiting for, the words she's been imagining for ten long years. He is coming to Johannesburg, and hopes his dear Bert will at least be able to get him from the station when he shows his freckled face in sunny South Africa, as promised! With jobs being scarce back in the USA, and Uncle Woolf's generous offer to help him with a visa, he can't think of a better time …

Bee is more than just a little excited. She writes back to her brother to tell him firstly how happy she is, and secondly to warn him that she's much fatter than when he last saw her. She's gone from 106 pounds to 130!

Eventually the day arrives. They drive to Johannesburg station. Bobby is nine years old and cannot wait to meet his Uncle Mike.

Waiting for the train to pull in makes for a slow half-hour. Phil and Bobby are sitting under a *Whites Only* sign on a bench when the distant thunder of wheels on tracks reaches them.

–*What if I don't recognise him?* Bee asks Phil anxiously.

–*Oh, you will.*

–*There he is! Oh my Lord, he is the handsomest brother in the world! Meyer!*

He is tall and lean and his acne is all gone; his hair is darker. His smile, thank goodness, is just the same as he picks his sister up off her feet and then looks at her. They stare into faces deeply familiar and yet changed.

–*Bert! You're the same as ever!*

–*You look like you've never been in the war!*

–*And you don't look fat at all!*

–*Bobby, come and say hi to Uncle Mike!*

Phil reaches out to shake Mike's hand first and is put at ease by his brother-in-law's warm American smile and dancing eyes.

–*Pleasure to meet you, Phil. Thank you for taking such good care of my sister*, he says. Then he turns to Bobby and picks him up in a bear hug.

This happiness was almost worth waiting for, Bee thinks. She can't stop looking at her brother. These are her people: her brother, her husband, her son.

–*I hope you like South Africa*, she says as they drive out of the city.

–*My sister's here, and her family. What could I not like about that?*

The first Sunday lunch with Mike at Aunt Dora and Uncle Woolf's happens on a rainy afternoon.

Life has come full circle. Bee's cousins are already half in love with Mike. At the table he raises his glass and proposes a toast:

–*To my beautiful sister, Bee, the prettiest girl in the world. And to my newly found family: Uncle Woolf, Aunt Dora and all the cousins. Thank you for waiting for me.*

In the corner of the room, Rose is fuming. Cultivating malice for almost a decade has not won her any ground. Bee is still at the centre, still eclipsing everyone. Last time she and Phil were here, Rose had come up to tell her Phil was stressed about business.

*–You'd do well to stop spending money on those fancy dresses and shoes, Bee. Your husband is about to collapse with the stress of it all.*

Bee refuses to even respond to her by now. It's nonsense. The store is fine and she makes all her own dresses anyway. Every single one.

Mildred and Joshua Lourie and their children are expected, but Bee knows they will cancel. It's been a long time since she's seen them. They have moved to Johannesburg, where Joshua has started a farming business. He has, some say, become a calculating and hardnosed businessman, resentful of most people. He eventually purchases a factory and all Bee knows is that he is very wealthy now and drives only the latest and greatest automobile.

*–And another toast*, says Uncle Woolf. *To my dear nephew Mike, the son of my late beloved sister. We are your family and you have come home. We will do everything we can to get your papers in order so that you can live happily ever after in South Africa.*

It is not as easy as he'd hoped. Mike's work visa is not granted and he has to leave the country after a few months. This is not how the story was supposed to unfold, especially as he's just fallen in love with a beautiful young actress. Bee is terrified he will go back to America, and in any other circumstance he may have. But his heart is now doubly bound to this burning continent. He cannot leave his sister and family, and certainly not the girl of his dreams. So he and Uncle Woolf hatch a plan: he goes to the neighbouring country of Swaziland, where he awaits the processing of his paperwork. He will end up living and working there for two years, an exile in Africa, visited sporadically by those he loves.

✡

The kiss with the German boy happens on a rainy afternoon. We are sitting on his bed and, outside, thunder rumbles across the sky and the light dims. The air is thick with the smell of wet earth. His drum kit is next to the bed, and as we laugh and joke, I slide off the bed and fall onto the pedal and the drum crash echoes behind our laughter. His arms are golden brown and he reaches down to help me back up again.

–*Noddy, you're hilarious,* he says.

His laughing eyes meet mine and I am terrified. I know it: no boy would ever kiss a girl he calls Noddy … but suddenly he is leaning over me, pressing his weight down on me, and his eyes tell a different story to his words, as our faces move closer together.

The heavens kiss the earth. Rain comes clattering down onto the tiled roof and his half-naked body presses mine into the single bed. The wet slasto outside reflects white light, and the German boy kisses the Jewish girl until she feels she might lose herself entirely.

✡

Over the two years that Mike is living in Swaziland, Bee falls pregnant seven times. Her bicornuate, heart-shaped uterus is a malformation she does not know she has. All the babies that are conceived attempt to grow in one of the small areas of the divided uterus and cannot develop very far before they are expelled. After so much heartbreak, she gives up hope of ever having more children.

And then, finally, her dear Mike is released from his exile in Swaziland. She is euphoric. All is as it is meant to be. He comes home to his family and his girlfriend. He finds work. The family is whole again.

When her period stops and she begins to gain weight she ignores her body. To avoid any disappointment, she also avoids the doctor.

One still afternoon, Mike is over at the house. It is as if he has always been there, and as if life has always been this perfect. While he is instructing twelve-year-old Bobby on the mechanics of automobile driving, Mike looks up at his sister from the living-room floor where they sit.

–*Bee! Gracious me, you're looking porky! What on earth have you been eating?*

–*Don't be rude, now!*

–*Well, you couldn't be PG now, could you?*

–*I doubt it*, she says.

–*Well, if you're not you should see the doc at any rate. Carrying that much weight can't be good for you.*

✡

In Chicago, Jacob stands in front of the window of Herschel's violin shop. His hand fumbles for the letter and he opens it, though he does not understand the English words he reads. He only knows what they mean because of the translation on the back written in Yiddish by the rabbi at shul. He walks into the shop, still reading the letter.

> Dear Grandpa Jacob,
>
> I hope you are well. I am writing to ask your advice and to let you know that I have a wish to learn the violin. My mother says you will be able to advise us which violin to buy so I can start to learn, because I understand you are a very good player yourself ... I hope to come and visit you in Chicago one day ...
>
> Love, your grandson, Bobby

He doesn't have enough money for the violin with the honey tones, but he chooses a half-size instrument with a sound like a warm summer evening, and asks Herschel to lower the bridge so that the E-string sits closer to the finger board. He also asks if Herschel can package up the violin carefully, as it will be taking a long journey to the other end of the world.

–*That'll cost extra, of course*, Herschel says.

–*Yes, of course. I understand.*

And when the violin arrives in South Africa months later, Bobby tears open the tightly wrapped parcel with his name on it.

Both he and Bee stare in disbelief.

–*Oh my! Bobby, your grandfather must really love you. He sent you a violin! Gosh, that's so unexpected. We have to write to him right away. You must treasure this forever, you hear?*

–*I will! I will! Can I have lessons? How soon can I start?*

–*We'll have to find a teacher, and ask your father for the money.*

✡

After thirteen years of dead babies and months of bed rest to keep this one inside, Bee goes into labour. The day is warm, and flies buzz lazily around the countertops in the kitchen when she rings Phil at work.

–*I think the baby's coming now. Please get home as fast as you can.*

Phil rushes home. He phones the hospital to tell them they're coming in. Then he hurries Bee into the car and puts his foot down flat. They fly down the bumpy roads, though Phil is not usually a speedy driver.

–*Help me*, Bee cries out.

He hits a pothole in the road and the baby's head crowns. Phil slams on the brakes and leans over in time to catch his newborn son in his arms.

At the hospital, when the emergency staff get to the car, they are surprised to find the baby cuddled against Bee's chest, the umbilical cord still attached to the placenta, which has not yet been expelled.

Once she has been formally admitted, Bee tells the nurses and the doctors:

–*You're not taking this baby from me for one blessed second. Everything you need to do, you do right here!*

–*Yes, ma'am*, says the nurse – young, unmatronly and without any backbone, thank God.

–*Thirteen years ago my baby died in this hospital. She would never have died if they had just left her by my side.*

–*They told me the records say jaundice. She died of jaundice, ma'am.*

–*Jaundice! She died because they took her away from me. You don't touch my Woody and you don't take him out of my sight.*

–*Yes, ma'am.*

✡

Woody (whose name is really Woolf, after his great-uncle) grows in the shade of his mother's devoted and sometimes overbearing love. By now, Bobby is a teenager and has decided to finish his matriculation at a boarding school an hour and a half's train ride from where they live. The violin sits in his cupboard at home unplayed. There wasn't enough money to commit to lessons, and now he's going away anyway.

One afternoon, Phil is waiting at the station to fetch Bobby. The train rolls in. The sun is hot in the sky, beating down on the cracked pavement. Phil can see his son's face against the window, and then, for some reason, the train doesn't stop. It rolls on out of the station. Phil feels an inexplicable terror. It has something to do with his son being pulled away from him. He races after the train, running as fast as he can along the platform, yelling at the top of his lungs.

–*Stop! Stop!*

But the train disappears. Phil battles to breathe and collapses on the rough paving.

✡

The general store is up for sale and then it sells. Things have been hard for a long while, but Phil has kept the details of his struggles to stay afloat carefully hidden from Bee. The price of this has been an impossible weight on his heart.

–*Phil has to take it easy,* Mike tells Bee. *He should take the job Joshua Lourie has offered him. You have to convince him of that, Bee. He's had one heart attack and he's not the youngest of men anymore.*

–*Mike, you know how stubborn he is. I wanted to buy some apartments with the money from the sale, but no, he wants to be in business. He's got some idea about going into business with Rose. Anyhow, he can't stand Joshua Lourie.*

*–No, it's really that Rose has some idea about going into business with Phil, and he's just going along with it. Tell him to give the job with Joshua a try. It's just managing a tyre shop or some such thing. He can do it.*

✡

On a Thursday afternoon, two weeks after my first kiss, the sky has cleared after a storm. Four o'clock and I've just finished my English homework. The phone rings.

*–Noddy?*

I'm so happy to hear his voice I can barely keep my voice even. Ninety-nine per cent of the time, I'm the caller, and he's the call-ee.

*–Hey, it's so great you called!*

*–Noddy, I have to tell you something.*

*–Okay.* Suddenly I can feel this is not a good thing.

*–I'm leaving. Going to boarding school in Pietermaritzburg.*

*–Oh. When?*

*–Next week.*

In the first year that he is away, he writes me eight letters. Most of them contain details of his daily life at boarding school, and he repeatedly tells me how homesick he is. These are not love letters, but every time I hold the small blue envelopes in front of me and read my name written in his even hand, I am a prisoner of my own blind love.

After almost ten months of being away, he returns for a long weekend and I go over to his house for lunch. I'm shaking. We haven't seen each other in all this time, but he's occupied every thought in my head, every space in my soul. I knock at the door and he opens it and smiles distantly. Then he gives me a hug without energy. He pats my back and avoids my eyes.

*–How've you been, Noddy, hey?*

*–Missing you every day*, I say. *You?*

*–Homesick, that's for sure. But I'm getting used to it.*

Is that supposed to mean something? I don't know. We spend a couple of hours with his parents in the living room, talking about nothing. They speak German to me, but he only speaks English.

*–Let's go for a swim*, he says to me at last.

*–I don't feel like it.*

*–Okay. Well, what do you feel like doing?*

*–Dunno. We could go for a walk by ourselves.*

*–Okay.*

We don't make it further than his mother's car, which is parked on the grass outside his house. We stand there for a moment, and then we sit with our backs against the warm metallic car doors.

*–I feel like you're not telling me stuff*, I say. *It's been, like, all these months and it's like you'd rather I wasn't here. I have no idea how you've really been, what you think, feel, especially about … us.*

*–I … don't want to hurt you.*

I can feel the weight of what is about to come down on me. It's all in slow motion though, and each moment stretches out to eternity so that I will always be able to relive it in bright technicolour, regardless of how hard I try to forget it.

*–It's just that I've never been in love with you. I love you as a friend, Noddy. But I'm trapped. I want to go out with other girls and be free and have fun.*

My chest heaves. A sob suffocates me. Right. How could I not have guessed this from the beginning? How could I have been so stupid as to believe, even for one insane moment, that this god of a human being would feel anything more than vague affection for someone who was such a hose? Noddy. Of course. While my face becomes a mess of snot and tears and dirt from the muddy grass

I am ripping out at the roots, I throw out one last line, one last plea to the universe, hoping that I am not utterly the victim of my own spectacular illusion-factory.

*–But that first time. The kiss. Was that real?*

Bugs tick in the afternoon. A flock of hadadas, those mournful Egyptian ibises, fly low overhead while he considers my question. After long moments he speaks.

*–Yes.*

I tell him I want to go home. And I get up and walk God-knows-where like some sort of madwoman, and he catches up with me and walks me back to the house and sits there quietly with me while I sob and wait for my mother to pick me up.

I imagine that as my heart shatters on my way home that Sunday afternoon, he is feeling a vague sense of relief, a sense of anticipation that when he gets back to boarding school he will no longer be carrying the image of the besotted Jewish girl as his inadvertent responsibility.

✡

Phil begins work for Joshua Lourie. The first evening he returns home and slams the newspaper down on the kitchen counter. Then he walks into the living room, where Bee is helping little Woody tidy up his blocks.

*–He's insufferable. Arrogant, heartless man. I should have followed my instincts and stayed well away from him.*

*–Please try to relax, Phil, dear. Here, have a glass of wine with your dinner and don't take him so seriously.*

Phil says nothing. He sips the red wine and stares into space. Woody comes to chatter to him but he ignores his son and drains his glass.

✡

To mark myself forever as a different person from the one who lost the German boy, I get my ears pierced. The pain of the piercing gun going into my earlobe defines the past as officially over.

I learn how to drive. My first car is a green Golf GTI that overheats every twenty minutes and threatens to explode in traffic. In my final exams at school, I achieve a rare thing: a high distinction in both English and German; the other German students in the country with similar grades are all native speakers.

As I drive home from my final exam, I am negotiating Johannesburg traffic on Bompass Road. The newspaper headlines are plastered to trees: *Bakkie-Driver Hijacked on Bompass Road.*

I think, *What a horrible thing to happen!* I don't know then that this is the beginning of a new wave. This is the first incident, and I'm there to see those first headlines. I don't know that over the next twenty-five years South Africans will be hijacked at a rate of fifty a day. The news of hijackings will be relegated from the front page to small, general articles about crime in South Africa on page four. And then, as hundreds of thousands of people lose their lives to violent crime, the papers will reach saturation point and turn their focus to other things. Car hijacking will be one of the most lucrative criminal activities, supported by the corrupt local police and by syndicates of professionals.

When that first ordinary citizen is hijacked, it is the beginning of payback for the sins of apartheid, which everyone has feared is inevitable. The retribution will affect everyone – the young, the old, weak and strong, rich and poor, white and black – but in the early 1990s we don't know that yet. We think of the hijacking as an isolated incident, not the beginning of some new wave of horror.

Our right-wing conservative government, with its roots firmly in the pro-Nazi Ossewabrandwag of the past, is nervous. It has been clamping down viciously on anti-apartheid activists for decades. We have death camps. But we're not supposed to know about them.

Nevertheless, I have a friend in the army – Special Forces, they call his department. He tells me that the guys he works with have free rein. They are trained in methods of torture. They are young, about nineteen, and sworn to secrecy. But not all of them can keep such secrets. In my teens, while sitting on the brown winter grass and throwing stones at the floating plastic in Emmarentia Dam, I learn some facts about detentions at John Vorster Square.

Men detained without trial die after swallowing bars of soap.

Sometimes they slip and fall from the tenth floor, which has limited access. Although reports state that these people have committed suicide, investigations reveal that their bodies show signs of torture.

At other times, they choke on tennis balls.

If an Indian detainee dies in detention, the police officers warn the black detainees to cooperate by reminding them that 'Indians can't fly'.

It is hard for me to breathe the air that so many dying citizens are breathing out.

Soldiers rush into the townships at night and kill the parents of sleeping children.

So when these children grow up they become hijackers and criminals – the ones who can say without blinking, to a white journalist:

*–I love my job. I'm prepared to die for it. I love crime. I tell people, I will put your baby in the oven if you don't give me your money. I cut the woman's throat just here, so that there's blood. I say I will finish this now, unless you give me your money.*

So, maybe it's no surprise that in the moment I read the headline about the hijacking, I contemplate how I might one day leave the country whose earth and sky I love. I begin to feel like I cannot belong to a place like this. There is even a sense of anger at the ignorance of my forebears.

I lack all courage. I'm not strong enough for this place and I know it.

✡

*–I've quit working for Joshua Lourie. I don't know what it is with that man. He seems to delight in making life as difficult as possible. I do the stocktaking and he puts me down. He finds fault with everything I do and has no respect for me at all. I won't stay anymore. I know he's married to your cousin and all that, but if he fell off the face of the earth I wouldn't be sorry.*

*–Phil, darling, you look tired. Come and sit down.*

*–Rose and I are going into business.*

*–I wish you wouldn't, Phil!*

*–What, you want me to keep working for that man? It'll kill me, you know! Are you crazy?*

*–Don't call me that!*

*–Oh, do be quiet now, will you?*

*–That's enough. I'm calling Mike.*

*–For God's sake, don't go calling Mike again …*

Mike has become Bee's lifeline. He lives in Johannesburg, near enough to visit every other weekend, and she is grateful that he is no longer living across the ocean. She imagines that he will come and get her and take her away for a while, until Phil promises to stop treating her like a child. He doesn't listen to her. Mike always listens. Bee marches to the phone and picks it up, pulling the cord hard across the table.

Bobby is in his room studying. His parents always fight. It's always about money and their voices knot his stomach. He hears his mother's sobbing voice.

*–Will you please come and get me, Mike? I can't take much more*

*of this! Please! Your own sister. You can't just leave me here! No, I'm not being unreasonable!*

✡

One after another, hearts give in. Uncle Woolf dies first. He has a stroke. Aunt Dora's own heart cannot bear the shock – so it falters, loses all capacity to keep her alive. She dies of heart failure soon after.

✡

In the wake of the loss of Woolf and Dora, Bee and Phil move from Groblersdal to the big city.

The business that Phil and Rose start is a fish and chips shop in Johannesburg. Importantly, Bee is now nearer to Mike and his wife, and their two sons, her nephews, which gives her comfort.

A beautiful garden backs onto the new house. Three large bedrooms look out onto a flowering jacaranda tree.

*–Don't you love this place, Bee darling?*

*–I do, Phil, of course. But I still think we should have bought those apartments. Those six flats – we could have rented them out and lived in one. It would have been a good investment.*

*–You can't possibly know anything about investments, darling. Really! I'm in business with Rose and things are going to get better.*

*–I sure hope so.*

Jacaranda blossoms make a halo of lilac at the foot of the tree. Bee looks up through the leaves at the arching sky. She loves the nature here, and the sprawling brick house and her two handsome sons. She is often sad that the familiar faces of Woolf and Dora are no longer part of her life. She tries to count her blessings, but at the deepest level of her soul, this place has never become entirely familiar, and the dispossessed and silent servants who say *yes madam* and *no madam* are there to remind her that she is a foreigner, whose position in society is one that hasn't been willingly given to her by the people.

✡

The new house is ready for a party, and Bee is anticipating the purchase of a piece of fabric to make a copy of an outfit she saw at Edgar's. In the evening she asks Phil at the dinner table for the money for the material.

–*Rose won't allow it*, Phil says, chewing on a tough piece of steak.

–*What do you mean she won't allow it?*

–*It's too expensive. We really have to watch our pennies.*

–*It's on sale, Phil! For goodness sake, it's just cloth!*

–*We only take money out of the register for essentials. That's not an essential.*

–*Well, I never!* Bee gets up from the table in disgust. She marches out of the room, watched silently by her husband and two sons.

If everyone lived on fish and chips in the early 1960s, Phil and Bee Davidow, and Rose with them, would have been wealthy indeed. But after eleven months, and because of bad positioning, and competition from other take-away places in the vicinity, business is poor.

–*I wish we'd never bought the stupid fish and chips business. I hate it.*

–*Darling, it's our bread and butter, don't say that.*

–*Well, why not? Who's it gonna hurt now? Rose gets more than her fair share and has the gumption to tell me I can't buy anything. Anything! I'm a poor woman in my own home. How do you think that feels?*

Phil doesn't get the chance to say how he feels. It feels awful. A lot like failure. It feels like a searing pain in the middle of his chest, a breaking of his heart. The end of his dreams.

✡

Mike is the last person to see him alive. The hospital corridor stinks of disinfectant. They are wheeling Phil away to intensive care and he is conscious. His face is grey. He raises his hand slightly and he looks at Mike.

✡

At forty-four, Bee becomes a widow. Woody is almost ten when his father dies. Bobby is studying pharmacology at the local university and has moved out of home. Not a week after Phil's death, Rose tells Bee:

*–We'll have to sell the shop. You'll have to get a job like everyone else. And there's a good Jewish orphanage down the road. I've talked with the others and they think it would be in Woody's best interests to go there. You can't be a mother and a breadwinner now.*

✡

Tuesday January 23, 1962

Dearest Bertha,

The thrill of your letter was quickly gone when I opened it and saw the dreadful news. I can't tell you how sorry I am that Phil is gone. I know how highly you thought of him through the years as you spoke only with praise. And what a big blow for Wolfie who is only 10 years young and has to become a man so soon. Thank goodness Phil saw one of his sons grown to manhood …

Love,
Gertrude

✡

At night the house is as lonely as a tomb. Dogs bark in the neighbourhood and Bee's heart is cold. If they had more money, Bobby could have been studying to be a doctor instead of a pharmacist. She so wanted him to be a doctor. That way they would have been rich, eventually. And he could have taken care of her. She knows now about her weak heart. A congenital defect, says the doctor. She fears her own death and wants her younger son to be properly taken care of.

She sits on the bed, strokes Woody's thick curls and tells him about the plan. Her words thud against the wall and die.

*–At the orphanage they would take care of you …*

His moan becomes a wail, then a scream. All the stories of the Ohio orphanage and his grandmother dying, and Mike and Bee as little children spending years and years with no parents to love them in the cold red buildings far away – all those stories are ricocheting through the head of the small boy who no longer has a father, and he kicks off his blankets and cries and cries into the night, until his voice goes hoarse and he begins to choke.

Bertha Frank Davidow does not put her son Woody in a Jewish orphanage. She lies awake in the darkness, and remembers the aching loneliness of a winter's night in Ohio. She remembers the childhood fears, the tears – most of all, she remembers the anguish of mother-loss.

She sits up in bed, her heart racing. She takes a glass of water in the dark and swallows a handful of pills. The doctor says she will need these all her life: some for angina, some for high blood pressure. Sobs shake her. She is furious with Rose: that evil thought would never have crossed her mind by itself. Bertha Frank Davidow will never be a mother who puts her son in a Jewish orphanage, no matter what.

✡

The fish and chips shop is finally sold – at a loss. Mike helps Bee sell the house and purchase a small apartment near Hillbrow. In four decades, the language on her street will be French. Her building will be hijacked by an organised Nigerian crime syndicate, and become a decaying squatter camp where illegal landlords arrive haphazardly to collect 'rent'. The land here will be one of the most violent places on earth.

But for now, the morning sun shines through large north-facing windows. Men in overalls hose down the pavement outside the building and weed the areas around the jacaranda trees. A double security gate at the entrance assures residents that they are safe from the poverty-stricken masses.

Bobby has his first job as a pharmacist and he sets aside money every month to support his mother and little brother.

And Bee gets a part-time position at Garlick's Department Store, in the scarves and neckwear department. It is twenty-two years since she left her job in America, but she steps into her position as if she has never been away from customer service, helping buyers select the best colours and fabrics that will go with their new fancy outfits.

✡

She comes home early from work one Friday to make a three-course dinner for her two sons.

She's not expecting Woody yet, and Bobby will only be home after five, so the knock at her door startles her and she runs to lock it with the chain – you never know these days. Then she peers through the peephole.

*–Who is it?*

*–It's me.*

All she can see is a black shirt. But the voice is familiar. She unlocks the chain, then the deadbolt, and turns the key.

She has not seen him for years. He was away on business for Phil's funeral. He might as well have vanished off the face of the earth. Until now. Joshua Lourie.

Grey streaks highlight his dark head of hair. His skin is still smooth. His eyes tell a story she would rather not see and he leans against the door.

*–Well, are you going to let me in?*

*–Oh, yes, yes of course. Hello, Joshua. This is rather a surprise.*

*–I'm sorry for your loss,* he says and walks past her without looking at her. He takes stock of the apartment, notes the chairs, the dark pine cabinet with all its trinkets. He surveys her domain like an estate agent. He doesn't at all seem sorry for her loss.

*–Can I get you anything? A cup of tea?*

*–Yes. Tea would be nice. You're expecting company later?*

*–Yes. My sons.*

*–Of course. Woody must be a big boy now.*

She looks at the broadness of his back. He takes out a cigar, lights it and blows a stinking ring into the middle of the living room.

*–Mind if I smoke.*

She turns her back on him to put the kettle on.

*–Despite life's tragedies, Bee, you're still a woman of grace.*

*–I'm not sure what you mean, Joshua, or what you want coming here like this.*

*–Well, try this, Bertha Frank: try waiting twenty-two years for the woman you love. Try living a half-truth, watching the woman you would do anything for go through so much pain, being unable to stop it, and yet knowing how different it could have been. Try longing with every part of your being every day of your life, for decades, for things to be different.*

Bee turns from the kettle and slams two cups down behind her on the lime-green kitchen counter. Her face, she knows, is beet-red. Her chest is heaving, and her eyes are full of unshed tears.

*–What in the world are you talking about, Joshua? I've lost my beloved husband, the man who gave me his whole heart and life, I have nothing left in the world but my two sons, and you come in here and tell me such things? You! A married man with grown children, married to my own cousin! How can you?*

*–My God, Bee, you're stubborn. Don't you see what I'm offering you? I love you, damn you. I've come here to humiliate myself and beg you to come to me. Still, after everything, I can't stop what I feel. I can help you. I want to take care of you and be with you for the rest of our lives.*

*–And my cousin Mildred? And your children?* She can hardly breathe.

*–I'll get a divorce. I'll make sure they're well taken care of, financially.*

*–Joshua, you must be the cruellest of men.*

She throws two teabags into a pot and pours the boiling water over them. It splashes onto her deformed hand and scalds the tiny fingers.

Joshua catches her in his arms from behind and covers her burned hand with his. He marches her over to the refrigerator, ripping open the freezer door. With a free hand he removes an ice-tray, bangs it onto the counter. Then he takes two cubes of ice and presses them over her burns. Melting shards lie like shattered glass on the floor.

–*You should have been mine*, he murmurs, reaching for a towel and blotting her fingers.

She looks up at his angular jaw, at the line of intensity that furrows his brow.

–*It's too late, Joshua. It was always too late.*

–*It's never too late*, he says, twenty-two years of anger and tears in his voice. She can't bear to see his face, so she closes her eyes. His arms slide up hers and she's sick from the pain in her fingers. He bends his head to kiss her, and as his hot breath blows against her face, she turns her head away.

–*For God's sake*, he growls. *What is your problem?*

–*My problem?* Her lips tremble. *My problem? My problem is that you, you're a married man. And for your information, I will always be true to my darling Phil, who was my husband, and whose memory I will never betray.*

Keys clatter and jingle against the door.

–*My son's home*, she says, wiping inadvertent tears from her cheeks.

Joshua stalks out of the kitchen and into the living room. As the young boy enters the room, he nods politely and moves swiftly past him out of the apartment.

–*What was* he *doing here, Mom?* Woody wrinkles his nose.

–*Paying us a visit.*

–*I'm glad he's not here for supper.*

–*Why, darling?*

–*I just don't like him.*

*I don't either*, Bee wants to say. But she can't. It would only be half the truth.

✡

It's taken me three years to be able to think of my German boy without my heart breaking. But I can do it now. While my friends have loved and lost over and over again, I have been unable to find anyone large enough to fill the vacuum left by my first love. That is, until I meet the university lecturer.

We are sitting on the tiled floor of Senate House at the University of the Witwatersrand, feeling like we are all at the centre of the universe as apartheid crumbles. In 1989, the campus is full of Black and Indian and White and Coloured students and we are all at one, defying the outrageous laws that have made such artificial divisions in our society for so many decades. We know that Mandela may be released from prison in the future. We know that we are in fact the most integrated society in the world, we just haven't been given the chance to show it yet. The atmosphere is electric. It's primed for people to fall in love. I am on the floor next to the coffee shop, and my friend Joao says:

*–You should meet Paul. He's a musician. And a writer. And he was a medic in the Rhodesian War. And everyone's apparently in love with him.*

And so, from the first moment, I'm compelled to look at this person opposite me as a coveted individual, and his soft-spoken manner is intriguing, and I start to like him and want to know about him. And I'm careful not to be too funny or jokey, so as not to be perceived merely as comic entertainment.

*–And there's a party at Paul's on Saturday. So you should come,* Joao announces.

*–No, there isn't,* Paul says.

*–There is now. Everyone here's invited. I'll bring the booze.*

I arrive early at Paul's flat in Yeoville and I think there's no one there. I want to say hi, but don't really mean to stay. I knock at the door and note the peeling paint, the grungy staircase to the second floor, and the music pounding rhythmically from the next-door flat.

I don't understand why I'm shaking when he opens the door.

–*Hi*, he says. *Come in. I didn't want this party, of course. But I'll chase them out early. Would you like a drink?*

–*Okay. What do you have?* Usually I can talk to anyone at any time, but it suddenly feels difficult. I wonder why he's telling me before the night has even begun that he'll chase them out early.

–*I don't have anything alcoholic. You'll have to wait for Joao for that. I can offer you tea and juice … or water.* He laughs, embarrassed.

–*It's fine. I don't really drink much at all.*

As we bond over cups of tea and raise them to our non-alcoholic status, my body wants to be near his. He tells me he wants to go to America and I tell him those are my sentiments exactly. We talk about what life would be like in a real democracy, where the majority of the population isn't starving and oppressed, and where everything is modern and First World. We talk about the land of opportunity until we can almost see it: a utopia where dreams can come true.

–*My gran was born there, you know. In Ohio. But I don't have any right of abode there … wish I did!*

–*Me too! If you had an American passport, I would marry you on the spot.*

Then he picks up his guitar and plays some of his own compositions.

His music is what my soul would write if it could. I had never imagined that falling in love could happen with one gesture, one look at his hand on the neck of the guitar. By the time people arrive, we are in a conversation bubble which lasts right through the evening. He tells me he's been recently hurt. He doesn't know if he can ever let anyone in again; he has put his heart behind a cold glass plate. But to me he feels warm. My skin, my heart, my body are all on fire.

Finally, one of his women friends in her late twenties pulls him aside. My ears are tuned in to her words above the music and wild laughter.

–*What are you doing with that nymphet? She can't be older than twelve.*

–*I think she's twenty,* he says.

–*A child, Paul. A child. You've been with her all night.*

–*And?*

–*And maybe you should admit there's something going on there.*

–*And so?*

She walks away, consumed by something bitter. I think it's time for me to go.

–*You're leaving?*

–*I should be going before it gets too late.*

–*You can stay over if you want to. I'm going to get rid of all these guys in a minute.*

I don't know what's got into me. I stay. The other woman stays too. It's one in the morning before she realises I'm not leaving and she gets up, hugs him, kisses him full on the lips while pressing her hips to his, says goodnight to him and then stomps out of the door into the night.

–*Whew,* he says. *I can make you a bed in the living room if you like.*

–*Okay.*

I'm helping him pull the sheet over the mattress and our heads are close together and he says, *It's cold tonight. You could just sleep in my bed.*

The music next door is still pounding faintly through the thick brick walls and I'm wearing one of his T-shirts under his Egyptian cotton sheets. We hug in the dark and I can feel he wants me.

–*This could be dangerous,* he says. *I don't know if I can love anyone again, and I don't want to hurt you.*

*–I don't care*, I say. *I'm pretty tough, really.* I sense I'm telling a lie, but it's a necessary one.

✡

When Granny Bee meets Paul she blushes. She whispers to me: *He has a nice jawline.*

✡

Ours is a marriage of convenience. He would have married me if I'd had an American passport, but I end up marrying him because he has a British passport and can get me out of South Africa on a student wife's visa. He's planning to go to the Midwest to finish his doctorate in America.

My dad, Bobby, is also planning to leave South Africa with his family. He's been granted Canadian residence and his wife and my younger siblings are getting ready to go. He's been trying to get Granny Bee to go with them, but although she has spent her life missing home, Canada is a foreign country too, and she's adamant that she cannot live in that kind of cold weather ever again.

At this point my father owns his own pharmacy, but it isn't doing very well. Essentially, he runs a not-for-profit organisation, and I've seen him at it. A young black man comes in with knife wounds and no money. Pharmacist Robert Jack Davidow treats his wounds and gives him a tube of triple antibiotic cream. The man clasps his hands in gratitude and leaves with the cream. A young Sotho mother who can't speak English comes in with her baby. She's totally distraught. The baby has diarrhoea and the benevolent pharmacist, who speaks her language, mixes her a kaolin remedy and sends her away. And on and on it goes.

Word gets around. Bob is soft-hearted. He's also highly intelligent and knows how to make mixtures for everything. He has a few paying customers but many others who can't afford the help he gives them. So it is not surprising that his business is on the brink of bankruptcy.

The night before he is due to leave for Canada, an unmarked van with four white Afrikaans policemen pulls up at my dad's house. They beat on the door. He opens it. They don't even speak to him. Broken thoughts and memories of the Ossewabrandwag ricochet in his heart. The neo-Nazis live on. The policemen grab him like he's not a living, feeling being, and they handcuff him and bundle him into the van.

–*What are you doing? My God! What are you doing?* My stepmother panics.

–*Liewe Hemel, mevrou. Don't pretend you know nothing. He owes money. Now we will teach you Jews a lesson. He's going to jail, that's what. No getting off to Canada for you fucking Jews.*

Shock reverberates into his body then and hides there, waiting to surface.

During the nights he spends in prison with hardened criminals, while his wife tries to negotiate with lawyers and I frantically place calls and pleas to every sector of society that I hope can help, trauma seeps into his limbs. In the leaden minutes where he sleeps with his wedding ring in his mouth so that his fingers won't be severed by other inmates, his soul is shattered. I cannot bear the hours, lying in my own bed in Johannesburg, knowing that he is in a cold prison cell. At night, my heart is a captive banging against my ribs, desperate for escape. I don't understand how this can happen to a soul that has done no harm, a soul full of kindness towards humanity.

And then, without warning, he is released. The charges are dropped. But his visa to Canada is cancelled forever, and something lives in him now that breaks his voice, which never properly recovers.

✡

In the months before Paul and I leave for America, my dad is held up at gunpoint three times. He tells me over the phone about the incident outside his house.

*–Sweetie, now don't be alarmed when I tell you this: I was held up yesterday. I was just closing the gate in the morning on my way to work, when this guy grabs me, bends my arms behind my back and puts a gun to my head.*

*–Oh, Dad!*

*–Well, he grabs the car keys and he asks for my gun and my wallet. I say, I don't own a bloody gun and I don't have my bloody wallet. He roughs me a bit, pats me down. Then he throws me forwards and gets into my car and drives away. You know the funny thing?*

*–I can't imagine!*

*–I did have my wallet. It was right there in my back pocket.*

*–Jeez, Dad! Why didn't you give it to him?*

*–Are you kidding me? I wasn't gonna give him my bloody wallet. It had all my credit cards, my other cards … I mean, what a hassle!*

*–But he had a gun to your head!*

*–Yes. He was an idiot.*

*–Dad, it's crazy, but you're a real hero for standing up to him.*

He survives again. The second time happens at night. When the thugs break in, they tie him and my stepmother up in the living room, and threaten to kill them if they so much as breathe.

Then the intruders make off with jewellery and other small valuables.

Just as my father and stepmother are recovering from this, they are held up again in broad afternoon light. They are at home with friends at the time. Because everything of any value has already been taken, the thieves relieve one of the visitors of her brand new car, and leave them, unbelievably, all with their lives intact.

I'm pretty sure America will be able to offer me a better life than this one, I think. And I imagine that if I get over there, maybe one day I will be able to save my whole Jewish African family from living in fear.

✡

We arrive as newlyweds in the Midwest, in a thickly humid summer. The air is so dense I can't breathe. Everywhere I turn my gaze, the architecture bears down on me – old and heavy, built by people who never knew the sun's equatorial power.

I am twenty-two years old and Paul is ten years older, and we have no idea that journeys have mirror images. I sense, but do not know, that this one is a reflection of another made so long before, by a 22-year-old American on her way to an unknown continent to marry a man ten years her senior, who would help her fulfil her dream of a better life. Perhaps, had I known, I might have learned the lesson about throwing yourself across the world in the hope of finding a better future.

As I look at the buildings built by Polish and German immigrants, I panic. I feel as though I'm suffocating.

*–This isn't what I thought America would be! I can't live here.*

*–What's the matter?*

*–I don't know. I just can't breathe. I feel like I died here.*

*–We'll be okay.*

The next morning we take a bus and rush to the hospital, because of the not-being-able-to-breathe situation.

After three hours on machines I am diagnosed with asthmatic bronchitis. The doctor also says:

*–What do you know about this heart murmur?*

*–Nothing.*

*–You should get it checked out.*

My lips turn blue.

We have never seen such an expensive hospital bill, so I do not go and check out the heart murmur.

A decade later I know it is a mitral valve prolapse. An inheritance waiting to be decoded.

Bertha Frank. I think of her growing up here, under these skies. Ethel. I think of her trying to breathe in this air at the end of her too-short life.

Eventually we find a tiny apartment made of cardboard. I've never experienced such thin walls. In South Africa, buildings are made of concrete blocks. The internal walls are so thick you could have a party at one end of a house and not wake sleeping parents at the other.

I cough and wheeze all night and I listen to neighbour number one below us tapping his toothbrush on the sink; neighbours numbers two and three upstairs making love morning and night on a squeaky bed; neighbour number four playing ear-shattering music to our left; and neighbour number five to our right yelling at his girlfriend.

As I lie on my bed staring at the ceiling of our boxy apartment, I realise that Ethel's grave is a few hours' drive to my left. To my right is the orphanage. I don't know if I can go there. Ever. Under these Midwestern skies, my great-grandmother died. If they would have had enough money, they could have managed to get her the care that would have saved her life. As I fight to breathe, I cannot bear the thought of her dying because she could not breathe. What was the last thing she saw? Was it the naked branches reaching skyward? Was it the inside of a musty room?

I walk along the banks of a grey lake as the leaves turn to gold and fall to the ground. Somewhere on the other side of the lake, the red brick walls of the former Jewish Orphan Home, where Meyer and Bertha Frank grew up, tower into the faded sky. Each year, the children watched the life die out of these autumn leaves as the summers flew by.

I think about the land to my west and the town of Hammond, Indiana; about a grave in the wind, visited by no one; about the tears of a ten-year-old girl as she stood there, disbelieving, while her mother was lowered into the earth. I am within driving distance of the house where she died. The graveyard is not far from the house; there lies Ethel Yalowitz Frank, and I am in her shadow.

Winter comes, and temperatures fall to twenty below zero. I shovel snow for five dollars an hour. I can't stay outside for more than ten minutes at a time. I clean apartments and vacuum the long mouldy passageways for a deduction in rent. I am a person of no particular status. My American dream dissolves.

We buy an old car for seven hundred dollars and drive south in the freezing drizzle. Chicago. The city looms over small immigrant people who are so insolent that they think they can come here to the land of opportunity and make it.

I am invisible in my overcoat as I walk the windy corridors between skyscrapers and look at the waters of Lake Michigan. I stop outside a large apartment building and imagine the lives lived inside, year after year, for nine months of cold. My chest feels heavy, as though someone is sitting on it.

And then he is there: the ghost of the man who was once a night-watchman behind these heavy doors – who stood here, night after night, playing every violin piece he knew in his head, to melt the hours away and keep the image of his dead wife and living children at bay. I am in the city of Jacob David Frank – his presence is in me as a weight that I cannot shake. This is his building. This is Chicago.

These are his steps and in the air are the whispers still from decades before – the prayers for his children, for a better life.

*–I need to leave here,* I tell Paul. *If I stay in the Midwest, I might die.*

But first I have to unravel something. The university building on the banks of Lake Michigan where Paul studies strikes fear into my chest whenever I look at it – and this reaction is beyond my comprehension. The imposing red brick front, the small windows and solid roof remind me of something I have never seen – in a place I must visit.

The Jewish Orphan Home in Cleveland, Ohio, is no longer Jewish, and no longer for orphans. Bellefaire does, however, offer help and care to children and teens who need it.

Michael Sharlitt's legacy lives on.

Bellefaire in the afternoon: on this path where I now stand, she once walked. This is the view she saw each day. And the main building, which looks out over the grounds, is a replica of the university building in Wisconsin where I have been for two winters. My hands tingle.

The ghost of a dead mother looks out from a top window and longs for her ageing children. I can feel her heart, and Bertha's younger heart, and a buried truth rises to the surface of my skin.

I *do* know this place. And yet I have never been here before. I have known these buildings only as apparitions in my deepest self as I grew up in South Africa, climbing trees with my mud-caked feet and unruly hair.

I follow the path under leafy arches towards the main entrance. The letter written by Gert to Bee many years ago comes alive again.

I remember once, when I printed some pictures of larger groups of kids, that I said something like "Forming childhood friendships which will last a lifetime." Yes, Bertha, the younger we are, the more stronger the ties. I can often remember just like yesterday, you and I walking around the campus, arm in arm, talking about our unknown future. We even used to look at the sticks (trees) just planted, looking so skinny against the large lawn, and wonder what they would look like in say 20 years. We realized they would probably form a nice archway across the walk. Well, it has been 20 years, and then another 20 years. And yes, they have long ago formed that archway across the walk, and whenever I look at these huge, strong trees, I do remember.

I remember the time, in confirmation cooking class, when you sprinkled salt into a cake or pie, instead of sugar. I remember lots of things, Bertha. Some, I feel guilty about, in the way kids can hurt eachother. But that is life. We grow up trying to find our own niche or personality, and without parents to help guide us we floundered. Some children were able to do this growing up and maturing quite successfully. I do not consider myself lucky enough to have been one of those chosen few.

Love, Gert.

Gertrude

On page 102 of the *Register of Orphans*, kept carefully inside the administration building of Bellefaire, I find two names and a date. The ink is brown and ageing and the names are in capitals.

FRANK, BERTHA
AGE: 11
FRANK, MEYER
AGE: 8-1
FORMER RESIDENCE: HAMMOND, INDIANA
DATE: NOV 17, 1927
FA: DAV FRANK, CLEVELAND, OHIO

My future was already written down the day Bertha and Meyer were placed here in the care of Jack Girick.

✡

After Phil dies, life in South Africa in the 1960s seems to become more dangerous, more unpredictable. Since March 1960, when African demonstrators were shot dead by police for protesting against unjust pass laws, Bee has felt a growing anxiety.

On the weekends, she manages life on her own by spending time with dear Mike and his family. It is on just such a weekend, as they are finishing a lunch of roast chicken and potatoes, that the river of destiny twists and begins to travel in an unexpected direction. Mike looks at his sister. She's eating a mouthful of potatoes.

*–Bee, I know this is going to come as a shock to you, but we've decided to go back to America. The recent riots in South Africa have shown us the writing on the wall. The Sharpeville event was the beginning of the end for us. We want our kids to grow up in a normal society.*

She swallows and stares at her brother across the floral tablecloth, which ripples in the spring breeze. Leaving. Mike and his family – going back to America. She fiddles with her wedding ring and blinks back tears.

*–I know you'll understand. And we'll be back to visit. Promise.*

She wants to sob and get down on her knees and beg her brother to take her and her boys with them, but it's impossible. She has nowhere to go. No money. No way to survive. Not even the airfare to get there.

*–Aren't you going to say anything, dear Bee?*

*–I just need some time,* she says. *Excuse me, Meyer.*

✡

Woody is with his cousins the day their mother takes them shopping for their move overseas. He watches with great envy the excitement of choosing new coats, the trying on of new shirts to be worn in a far-off land – his mother's land. He stands there on the side, unnoticed, bearing witness to the act that will leave him behind.

✡

Bee receives a postcard from London, written hastily en route. But by this time Mike has already arrived back in America. She looks out at the oak trees along the pavement. In the early morning light, they have halos. The single reason for living is an upcoming wedding: Bobby has met a beautiful girl from a nice Jewish family. Her name is Carol.

✡

The phone rings on a Saturday morning and when she picks it up, she's surprised to hear her brother on the other line.

*–Bee? It's me.*

*–How are you, Mike? Boy, you sure took a long time to let me hear your voice.*

*–Bee, I'm sorry. It's bad news. Dad passed away two days ago in Chicago. His landlady said he hadn't been very well for some time. I don't know what the financial situation is, but I'll let you know as soon as I do. There may be something left for us, but don't have any expectations.*

Bee feels the breeze through the open window carry echoes of her past across the room. She has lived so many lives since her mother's death. Phil is gone. Mike is back in America, and her father has died alone, in a small room in an apartment near the edge of Lake Michigan. The dream of her own future, which she once held so tightly in her heart, is dispersing into memories of what once was.

May 16, 1968

Dear Bee:

My letter of yesterday was a bit hurried and this one will be short too. What I want to tell you is that I had to tell the attorney about the State Pension business and he told me at first that he didn't think it would matter, which is what I told you, but after going into it he advised me much as I feared that the estate will have a big claim against it. It would appear that the State paid ~~xxxx~~ Dad about $7500 and after you consider the various expenses involved in settling it there probably won't be too much left. We now have to figure on this basis because he says that they pretty well cross check these things out and they will almost certainly turn it up. So, don't count on ~~xx~~ too much and we won't be disappointed. I do hope that you will at least get enough to make a trip here. I am certain that has been a dream of yours all your life and if you can at least do that then all of Dad's savings will not have been totally in vain. I'll keep you informed of what the situation is. I actually wanted to spare you the anxiety of the ups and downs but I feel you really would to know about the events and possibilities as they occur.

Love

Mike

✡

In the wedding pictures, the groom is handsome. He looks like Clark Kent in the early *Superman* movies with his thick-rimmed glasses. Courage has a quiet face; it is the sound that anyone might miss at a casual glance. But it's already there, forty-five years before it will show its truth, in the smile and the gentle hands. The bride is eighteen and her almond eyes are hungry for the future. Bee's hat looks like a cake. She's dressed in Prussian blue, the happiest dress she's worn since her wedding day. Above the wedding party, in the sky, the Egyptian ibises call the future towards them.

Their honeymoon, like Bee's honeymoon, is in Lourenço Marques. The sea is an aquamarine blue and Mozambique trembles on the edge of war.

✡

April 11, 1969: on the sides of the road, white and pink cosmos flowers line the tarmac. They smile in the cool autumn winds. Bee asks Woody to please drive faster so that they can get to the hospital already.

A girl. A granddaughter. Someone to love. Someone new in the world to love her back.

–*My little girl*, she says in the white ward.

–*We're just going to bathe her*, says the nurse to the young mother. The mother-in-law throws a tantrum.

–*Don't you take that baby away from its mother!*

–*Leave her with me, please*, says the mother.

The nurse looks from the mother to the father to the grandmother and the gangly young uncle. What is wrong with these people? She walks smartly out of the room and comes back with the head nurse to get this baby bathed, for goodness sake!

Bee fears the notorious Angel of Death is hovering nearby. She assumes it's there because she feels it, waiting to take her granddaughter. But the Angel is merciful. He leaves me, Bee's first grandchild, to live, satisfying himself that he will take the next one, a little boy, less than three years hence.

✡

South Africa through the eyes of a ten-month-old is a haze of intoxicating smells and colours that burn themselves into the soul. I sit outside in a feeding chair and play with the leaves of a geranium bush that my mom has put on the plastic table in front of me. Sometimes when I look up at the sky, I see enormous worlds hanging from strings. They stun me with their beauty. At night, though, when I lie in my cot, a huge force picks me up and holds me prisoner above my curtains. When I try to cry, the force takes my voice away.

Mornings are always the beginning of the world. I am whole, lying on a blanket on the lawn, drinking a bottle of milk. I love my mom excessively, because she's so funny. She puts my hat over her face and it seems like she's gone. But then she always comes back and both of us laugh. I know she goes to art classes in the afternoons and the sound of her car driving away means emptiness. I cannot bear her absence and panic pulses through me. My hearing is attuned to the sound of her car coming home, and when I know she is back, the universe is in order.

Sometimes, both my mom and my dad kiss me goodnight. In those moments, when both of them are in my room, the tumult in my blood is quiet. My house in Norwood, Johannesburg, has a Home Tree, a giant oak marking the spot where I live, rooting me to my place of birth. It will outlive most of the inhabitants on the street.

Forty-five years later the tree is still there, but in 2014 the garden, once surrounded by a rickety split-pole fence, has a ten-foot-high concrete wall with electrified razor wire on top. The wall's not completely burglar proof, but it does help. If someone wants to get in, they just need to scale the wall, use string to hold the wire apart and get someone through.

But the world when I am a toddler seems to be a more innocent place, and fear has not yet solidified into a stone under my heart.

In the afternoon, the sky is as blue as dreams and the clouds are touched with pink. People walk past the fence talking, laughing, as they walk down the pavement, their brightly coloured clothing catching my eye through the wooden slats as they make their way towards the African compound at the end of the street. My eyes and ears catch only the colours, the beauty, the warmth and familiarity of Zulu and Tswana being shouted across the streets, and not the underlying reality of a country on the brink of a violent civil revolution.

*–Granny Bee, I want my mom.*

*–She's at the hospital, darling.*

*–Then I want my dad.*

*–He's there too, darling. They're going to be home soon. They'll bring back the new baby from the hospital and we will hug it and kiss it and put it in the new crib.*

The sound of the car arriving is a relief. I climb down the verandah steps and run to the edge of the lawn. But when my dad turns off the engine and gets out of the car, he doesn't pick me up and throw me high into the sky.

My mother has no smile and her arms are empty. In the back of the car, the new carry-cot holds only nappies and Baby-Gros.

The angels took the baby back to heaven.

That insatiable Angel of Death who has been taking babies from this family for decades.

My father walks into the house. He, at least, got to hold his dead son. But my mother didn't. They knocked her out with a shot, she says later. After they lost the heartbeat. Forty years into the future she will tell me, *I can still cry for him, that baby.* But my father got to hold the tiny limp body with the deformed legs and the cherub face. He kissed the head and let his tears fall onto the closed eyes of the boy who never lived.

He sits down on the fabric couch and stares at the encroaching shadows on the wall.

A week or two later Granny Bee brings me a present from the shoe department at Garlick's. She takes two fluffy things out of a paper bag. I don't know what they are, but I think I love them already.

–*Slippers*, Granny Bee says. She holds them up and jiggles them. Then I notice that each slipper has two beady eyes that rattle around. Monstrous. I run into the house as fast as I can to find my mother.

Eyes are everywhere. They stare at me from the walls when I want to sleep at night. I can see them looking down at me from the pattern in my curtains. Just as I'm falling asleep, big heads with eyes in them leap around the side of my bed. They look like black flames that move and change. The heads are like dogs' heads, but the eyes are more like people's.

For a while I think the slippers are gone forever. Then one morning I slide off my bed and creep under it to collect my bear, Downy, who has fallen there overnight. I am suddenly face to face with two sets of staring eyes. They peer at me, full of menace, and I dissolve into such terrified screams that my mother rushes into the room.

*–What's the matter, love? What is the matter?*

*–There's dead babies under the bed,* I scream.

She locates the slippers and holds them up. I bury my face in her warm brown hair. I cannot look at them, those holy terrors.

*–They're just slippers, Shell. Look, the eyes are plastic and they're silly. We'll throw them away, and when the rubbish man comes to take the rubbish, you will see him drive off with those silly,* silly *things in the back of the truck.*

I don't look at them. I like the word 'silly'. I hear the thuds as they go into the plastic bin in the kitchen. I love my mother forever.

✡

When I fall in love with the medic-musician, I do not know that the music he composes will write itself into the future.

✡

Midwinter, the Midwest, USA. Wind chill sends the temperatures plummeting to seventy below zero. The windows of the small apartment ice over on the inside. I fight for each breath and I feel that I am living someone else's life. I know these cracked streets and the smell of Kentucky Fried Chicken in the freezing air. And my African self rebels against the confines of an obliterating winter. I stare out at the empty street where no one would dare walk. The trees are bare sticks against a white sky. The dirty snow has frozen solid on the sides of the road. Every living creature has fled this annihilating cold, except for us. I am an African transplant poorly equipped for the Midwest. I have no right of abode, no right to work, no right to go to the hospital if I can't breathe. In this, the land of my grandmother's birth, I am a foreigner, an invisible new arrival with a heart full of ideals that are rapidly crumbling. The weight that is on my chest has taken on a recognisable form, and I can see the shadow I wish to escape.

I dream of dead babies. Night after night I hold tiny withered children in the palm of my hand. One of them is a boy. His skin is see-through and he's the size of a mouse. He's desperately hungry and he holds on to my finger for dear life and he's too small to eat anything, so I know he's going to die. I rush out of a room, calling for help, but already it is too late and the baby lies dead in my hand. I wake up and whisper to Paul, *We cannot have children in America.*

✡

By the time my mother is twenty-four, she has two small children. A year after my dead brother, another baby is born. Larry has a solid hold on life. I protect him with a bossy and fierce love. But my mother has a whole life ahead of her. Getting married was just a step out of home. Having children was another. The next step is waiting for her, and it looks completely different to the traditional life she was beginning to lead. She has fallen in love with someone else.

My father is made of soft material. Even in his late twenties, his head is bent forward as he walks, as though he carries something heavy. His departure is silent and causes very few ripples. But the heart of a four-year-old is still the size of a universe made up of two beloved parents, and when one leaves, no matter how quietly, the universe is forever torn in two.

Years later, just before I leave for America, my father tells me:

*–Your mother was my first love, and as such, I will always have a special place for her in my heart. When she left me, the only thing that kept me from doing myself in was the fact that I had two young children in the world.*

✡

All through the 1970s and into the 1980s, every Sunday Granny Bee and Uncle Woody come to visit us. My mother has remarried and I have two new brothers. My father has also remarried, and I have another brother and a sister. Granny Bee disapproves of everything that has happened. She is terrified of losing us, her first grandchildren, and she blames my mother for making rash and immature decisions, and for not understanding that marriage is a binding contract that one never abandons for any reason – least of all, falling in love with someone else.

✡

Sometimes, when I lie on the winter grass and close my eyes, I can hear whole orchestras playing just outside my head. They play pieces I recognise, but occasionally they go off on their own and deliver the most moving, intricate pieces that are entirely beyond my control. Above all the instruments, I hear the music of the imaginary violins.

They seem real, though I'm sure no one else can hear them. This is when I tell my family that I dream of being a violin-player and I learn that Granny Bee still has the violin that my great-grandfather Jacob gave to my dad.

And so begins my short-lived career as a violinist, under the tutelage of the renowned Mr Miller.

✡

One afternoon, Bee is arriving home from work. The 1970s are proving to be more unstable than even the 1960s. She is thinking about the weekend, about the visit to her grandchildren. She doesn't drive, so Woody will have to take her. He wanted to go out with his friends, but she has been adamant that these visits must take priority. She walks the few steps through the security door of her apartment and stands to face the lift.

*–Hey, old lady!*

*–Hey, you piece of shit-white oppression!*

She sees their young black faces curled in matching snarls. Their eyes are the substance of hatred. The first one grabs her and knees her in the stomach. She folds over. The first leaden blow hits her head; the cold tiles on the floor next to the lift hit her cheek as she crashes to the ground.

The young men grab her bag and run. At the corner of the street they rummage through her stuff and tear open her purse.

They find fifty cents.

One of the men pockets the money and tosses the bag into the gutter.

Time disappears. She is a small girl pulling a cart with her baby brother in it, in Hammond, Indiana, listening to the sound of her father playing the violin inside the house. She is freezing in the old orphanage at night and missing her mother. She is walking around London with Gainor, and because she knows she will never see him again, she can see in great detail the light in his eyes, the expansive generosity of his hands which hover around her as she crosses the street. She is at her daughter's gravesite and the smell of decay and death is everywhere. She is crying for Phil to come and get her out of this but all the while she knows he is dead.

When she opens her eyes she is sobbing and terrified: the kind face staring into hers is the colour of a deep brown river.

*–Just try to take it easy, Mrs Davidow. You are lucky to be alive. How is your head feeling?*

*–My head?*

*–Yes. It was quite a blow to the head. We feared internal bleeding.*

*–My head aches. Did they catch them?*

The nurse shakes her head. Bee does not want this nurse. Why are there black nurses now in a white hospital? Where are the young Afrikaans nurses she is used to seeing? Something is wrong. The nurse's skin is a reminder of her terror.

*–Not all black people want to hurt white people, Mrs Davidow. Most of us are decent people, just like most of you white people are decent people.* She speaks kindly. Her English is perfect.

Bertha turns her head away from the mind-reading young nurse and it throbs like the thunder of African war drums.

✡

She is grateful to hear from Gert when she finally gets home, but then there's so much she cannot explain.

> I read your letter to Jean over the phone last night, and she was grateful to me. She felt so bad when I told her about your mugging.

In fact, she was horrified, as I am! Would it be better for you to live elsewhere? How about when Woolf finally moves away. Could you rent a nice room in a classy house someplace? Are your suburbs like ours here? By that, I mean, our suburbs get nicer the further away from the central city you get. At one time, Cleveland Hts. was pretty elegant. Remember? Well, then came University Hts. and Shaker, then Beachwood and then Pepper Pike. And you should see the large homes and grounds in Pepper Pike!!!

✡

South Africa's nationalist party is digging in its heels and holding on tight to white western civilisation. In June 1976, the National Party decrees that all black and coloured students will now be instructed in the language of the oppressor: Afrikaans. And then all hell breaks loose. Children run out of their schools with bricks and stones and matches. They smash shops and station windows and they are ready to die for the freedom to be autonomous human beings. And the police open fire on them, on children as young as I am.

I am seven years old, standing on a station platform, waiting to catch a train home from school. Granny Bee is still in hospital after her attack. When I get onto the train, the carriages are almost empty. The train flies through stations. My stop is forty minutes down the track at the end of the line and as we thunder past yet another station, I stretch my head out of the open window to read the sign, and to see where we are. As I do so, a young coloured boy on the platform raises his satchel and slams it into my face, yelling at me.

*–Whitey!*

I stumble back with a numb face and a blood nose; this is a taste of the complex nature of South African society – someone who doesn't even know you can hate you. I don't understand this.

In her hospital bed, Bee comprehends it even less. She is Jewish. She carries the shadows of Jacob and Ethel in her blood more deeply than the whiteman shadows of apartheid South Africa.

✡

In the freezing Midwestern winter, my soul unravels. The ground is bare and the landscape is empty of all colour. And for nine long human months, I fight to breathe in deeply and even harder to breathe out, and I stare at the same leafless tree in front of the apartment complex; I wonder at the capacity of human beings to live this rats'-nest existence in a small, noisy cardboard box. I am trapped in a shadow of the past and I can't escape it. I wonder at the obtuse nature of fortune: I wish I had American citizenship. Or even permanent residence. I see that I will never be able to rescue my family from South Africa. I wish I were something other than the wife of a student in a bleak Midwestern town. I wish Granny Bee had been able to give to my dad and to me the gift of being able to belong here.

Jacob came to America so that his children and grandchildren would not have to suffer displacement. But the future is always written in an uncertain hand.

I think back to my life beneath an almost equatorial sun: the smell of autumn dust and lawn, the day my German boy broke my heart. I wonder at the power of dreams to move human beings such vast distances across the planet.

✡

Some months after the attack, when the physical scars have mostly healed and only one small mark remains at the back of her head, Bee receives a letter from Joshua Lourie.

He writes to express his sincere regret at the appalling attack on her person. He has not been well or he would have come to visit. He knows that she may very well not think highly of him, but he begs her to visit him, if there is any way she can afford the time.

She could ask Woody to drive her there, but she thinks better of it. She finishes work at Garlick's early, and takes a taxi to the leafy suburb of Sydenham. Most of the houses have alarms and burglar bars, but the fences are still low enough to see in. A large syringa tree scatters hard yellow berries along the slasto path to the house. Overhead, a thick roll of cloud threatens rain.

She rings the doorbell.

The maid lets her in and calls over her shoulder, *She's here, Baas.* In a few short years that kind of terminology will vanish from everyone's lips. But for now it doesn't even make Bee blink.

She follows the maid into the living room. In a dark corner, beneath a disjointed Picasso print, an old man sits in a chair. He has a blanket over his knees and the room smells like mothballs. Outside, the sun turns the world to evening gold and thunder shakes the windowpanes.

*–Oh my God. You came. Thank you. Thank you.*

His face is the same, but the firm line of his jaw has sagged and the hollows beneath his eyes seem bruised. He's not as old as he looks and Bee searches his face for the steely arrogance she knows so well.

*–How are you, Joshua?* She pulls up a dining room chair so that she's close to him, so that their knees almost touch.

*–Just as you can see. The details I won't bore you with. More importantly, how are you?*

*–I'm just fine, thank you.*

He grumbles something. Then he says: *Did they ever catch your attackers?*

*–No. I'm lucky to be alive, the doctors said. They'd left me for dead.*

*–I would like to kill them with my bare hands*, he says. She sees the flicker of his former self light his eyes for a moment. *Bee. Indulge me, please. I need to say something, to ask something …*

She leans in closer. He reaches out a hand, which trembles, and he holds it open.

*–I need forgiveness. For everything. I have been a heartless rascal. And I've ruined myself. God, the way I imposed myself on you … from the beginning. Shameless. Utterly. The way I assumed that … that you were too good for Phil and yet good enough for me. The cheek of it … the pain I caused. The way I married your cousin and made her miserable.* He begins to cough, or perhaps he is trying not to cry. He fumbles for a handkerchief in his pocket and blows his nose. *Well, I've been a heartless brute, Bee. And my comeuppance has come. I am penniless, sick, and I cannot hold my head up. I don't deserve the respect of my wife and children. And if I die without your forgiveness, I will live in an eternal hell. Tell me, dear, sweet Bee … can you forgive …*

His voice breaks and his face crumples. Bee is so stunned at his tears she can't move at all.

*–Oh, if you can't, I do understand. It's … How should I expect you to …*

She leans across suddenly. She takes his outstretched hand and holds it. In her heart, something opens, but it no longer has the power of a wave crashing over rocks at high tide. It is the softness of a setting sun through the clouds, through the curtains, bathing everything in fading light.

*–Yes, Joshua, you have my forgiveness. If there is anything to forgive.*

She thinks of her dead daughter and the coffin. In the amber light drenching the room, she sees in his eyes, for a moment, the man he was – and the man he could have been. And then he shakes his head. He cradles her hand in his, and brings it close to his heart and his tears fall readily, as the sky breaks outside and rain splatters on the corrugated-iron roof.

–*If I had my life over*, he says, his voice unrecognisable, *I would do things differently. You have been such a good person, my dear Bee. I would not have been such an arrogant cad. I would have been gentler, kinder, but I was ... overcome by my own desires and I could not see then, that if I would have won you I would never have deserved you ...*

–*Hush now, Joshua. You don't have to say any more. If God had meant it to be another way, he would have made it happen. Of that I must be certain.*

And when Bee leaves in the twilight, the storm clears. Her taxi pulls up to take her home and she senses that she will never see Joshua Lourie again.

✡

On the front page of the newspaper Bee reads about another death in detention. South Africa has become a dangerous place, even for walking, or catching buses and taxis. She fears all black people. Sometimes she's terrified she sees the same thugs who beat her almost to death. And she doesn't want to believe what people are telling her: that what the South African police force is doing to black people is no different from what the Nazis did to the Jews in the Holocaust; that many Afrikaners are white supremacist neo-Nazis who would be quite happy to exterminate all dark-skinned people, including Jews. There are rumours of death squads and death camps. Can it be true that the police are throwing detainees out of the ninth-floor window in John Vorster Square? These pictures don't make sense when she wakes in the morning to joyful birdsong and bright sunlight. She wishes for normality with all her heart. For a reprieve from heaviness.

When the letter arrives from Gert, it is as though someone has thrown her a lifeline. She sits in her flat and rests her aching feet on an opposite chair. She has no idea how much longer she will be able to keep working. But here is something surprising. Unimaginable.

The Jewish Orphan Home Alumni are going to have their fiftieth-anniversary reunion. Gert is making plans to bring her over and hopes she will accept: they will organise her ticket, her accommodation and anything else she needs. Bertha can scarcely believe it. She feels her spirits lift.

✡

In fifty years, the trees along the pathway to the large red brick building have arched over and created a shady tunnel. The cottages are covered with ivy. They seem so small. The humid summer air is laden with the weight of the past.

*–Bert! Bert! It's us!*

She might be forgiven for not recognising the two old women coming towards her. Their bodies are unrecognisable. It's only when she's right up close that their faces give them away. Behind the layers of fine lines and the strange hairstyles, she can see them emerging from the past.

*–Oh my Lord, Gert! Oh, Arleen. You look just the same!*

*–Oh, Bert, how do you do it? Look at her, Gert. Not even a wrinkle.*

*–Ladies, we've changed,* Bee laughs. *Gotta face facts. We're over seventy!*

Arleen still stands up straight. Her cropped grey hair frames her familiar face. Gert is fatter than Bee remembers her being, but then again, she realises, so is she. They are like the trees. Willowy, supple youth has been replaced by wide and barky age. Bee looks at Gert, takes note of her eyes, her smile, the way life has carved her face. Four children, a divorce. Grandchildren.

And Arleen: perhaps she has changed the least out of the three of them. Her eyes still dance with laughter. She's never married, never had children. She links her arm through each of theirs and they walk like that, beneath the halo of summer trees, towards the grand entrance of the main building.

*–I wanted to say, last time we saw each other none of us had a man in our lives. Fifty years on, and here we are again. No men, just us. And the children, and the grandkids.* Gert walks slowly. Impossible to tell now, that she will outlive her friends; that nearly thirty years later, she will be alive and well in her late nineties.

*–I always wanted to know why you never married again after Leon,* Bee says.

*–One marriage was more than enough. You know, you make some mistakes, and because you're doing the best you can and don't have any good examples to live by, it's all trial and error. And so the errors were made and I didn't see the point in going through any of that kind of stuff again. I was better off on my own. What about you, after Phil? You were still young.*

*–I had the opportunity but I turned it away.* In five minutes, as they ascend the steps to the main building one last time, Bee tells her two oldest friends about Joshua Lourie.

*–You're a good person, Bee,* Arleen says. *I guess you really did love your Phil. Not having been married myself, and never having wanted a man in my life, I can understand wanting to be alone better than I understand any other position. Though I might say this now, I had such a crush on Meyer when he was about fourteen. Is Meyer coming to the reunion?*

*–Sure is! And he calls himself Mike now, by the way. You didn't really have a crush on him, though, did you, Arleen?*

*–Of course I did. He was so charming.*

*–His face was full of zits!* Bee laughs.

*–Of course it was! But what did that matter? Oh, we were so young then, Bert. I wish we could do this again all over.*

The big building smells just the same. There is the pungent musty aroma of summer. But the emptiness in the hallway echoes around their footsteps.

The dining hall fills slowly with men and women, talking softly, laughing. For some, there are tears. Heads are bent. Hair is grey, or white, or non-existent.

*–There's Meyer!*

Peter Pan–like, Mike crosses the floor and hugs his sister so tight she can hardly breathe. Then he turns to hug Arleen and Gert.

Bee cannot swallow down the choking heartbreak. There was once a dream: that she would go to Africa and marry Phil, and that Meyer would join her eventually, and they would all live happily ever after. And the years have gone by and all that she imagined did come to pass, though so much more that was unimaginable happened. And she has come full circle. She is back beneath the roof of the only place which, despite its shadows, felt like home. And she cannot return to the past – to all that was. The passage of time haunts her.

Because this moment *is* happily ever after – everyone coming to the sunset years of their lives, with their narratives, their memories, their dreams; this is the ever after of Meyer and Bertha Frank, children of Jacob and Ethel: Mike is living back in America, happy, healthy and as unaffected as if he'd never left. Fifty years after leaving America penniless, Bee is still so poor that without the support of Bobby, she could not survive.

She is a survivor, though, not just of a brutal attack, but of permanent displacement. Of heartbreak.

At dinner, Arleen, sitting next to her as they tuck into some old favourites like heavy ice-cream, says:

*–Bert, out of everyone, you are the most changed, for the better. Life has made you rich. Deep. You've suffered. You've experienced the real world. Too many of us are just fixated on the most pedantic of things. But you … you've elevated yourself beyond that. I admire you.*

In the late moonlight, after dinner, the men and women, bowed with age, walk through the grounds to the cottages. Not every one of them is there. So many have gone. She had no idea how much loss there was during the war. Bee doesn't know this until she hears the conversations: someone's younger brother died; another lost a fiance; and then there were the families devastated by the Nazis.

*–Al was lost in the last weeks of the war, when the end was already in sight.*

Al!

*–Abe was shot down on D-Day. I'll never forget … I don't know that the sadness will ever go. He used to spy on us from that cottage. He told me that when we got engaged.*

Bee walks close to Arleen and Gert. There, in their moonlit reflections in the cottage windows, are the ghosts of small faces. They look out into a future and wonder what it will hold for them. The pairs of eyes staring back at their younger selves are misting over. Time has taken them on its irrevocable journey. Their hearts are the same. For some, memories are beginning to fade. Only the most momentous remain. The day-to-day details of the Jewish Orphan Home are evaporating into whispers. In her head, as they walk between the cottages, Bee hears the organ playing Handel's *Largo.*

*–I think it's time to be going,* she says, and turns back to the main building.

✡

When Bee leaves America for the last time, she holds pictures of Gert and Arleen close. She focuses on the warmth of the Southern Hemisphere sun, and on her sons, her grandchildren. The flights back to Africa take more than twenty-four hours. And yet this retracing of her journey seems far too quick: an eight-hour flight from the east coast of the USA to England seems incomprehensible compared with the many days aboard the SS *Berengaria.* She looks down from the air at the city of London and remembers a young man, and how much her heart might have felt, had she allowed it to. Even the twelve hours travelling back to Johannesburg seem to melt away quickly. She is a spark of light vanishing into darkness. Her once limitless circle of people and dreams has diminished into something almost invisible.

✡

I watch the hands of my musician-medic husband as they turn pale in the winter light of another year. I don't feel I know him anymore in this place. When I go downstairs to get mail from our letterbox, I feel that the life I am living belongs to someone else. I am not this sad person in a big winter coat who cannot breathe and who must carry Ventolin wherever she goes.

Paul finishes his PhD. I fall pregnant in 1996. I know that I have to go back to Africa to have the baby. We do not have permanent residence in America and I know that we cannot have children in a place where the air itself is suffocation.

✡

My son is born in South Africa. He comes into the world on an early spring afternoon in Johannesburg in 1997. Pushing one human body out of another one is an impossible feat. Birth and death are separated by a thin veil of chance. I understand how easy it would be to just die, the pain is so great … until broken, and torn, I hold my newborn son against my heart. Paul's eyes are full of tears, but mine are dry. For a while I feel as though I have left this body, and cannot be in it. Then my baby's tiny hands scratch my skin and I note the length of his fingers, the strength of them. I wrap my arms around him and make a vow to the universe: I will never do this again. I will protect this child from all harm, so that he might live to a very old age. The ache for his well-being is more than I can bear.

Paul drives us to my mother and stepfather's house and I sit at the back of the car with the baby held tight against me. The tears that I cry are for the lost children, for my dead brother. And the car seat is empty, because my plan is that if the car is hijacked, I will hold my son close, open the door, and roll us out onto the road. My body is still torn and bleeding and I don't know how I would make such a daring escape, but I have become, now, an animal protector of another life and I would risk mine for his without question.

A few nights later, the property is invaded. Dogs bark. I am filled with panic, with life-or-death fear. The sense that you may, in a few minutes, be dead. The terror of having someone to protect is the most paralysing of all.

I have rehearsed this moment. I pick up the phone and dial the emergency police number.

*–Can you please get here as soon as possible? We have eleven or maybe twelve intruders walking through the property.*

*–Ma'am, I can't. We don't have anyone at the police station to take fingerprints.*

*–I don't care about fingerprints. Our lives are in danger. I've just had a baby, can you get over here quickly?* My voice is commanding, and he says he'll be there.

He's as good as his word. The twentysomething-year-old Zulu policeman arrives on his own without backup. The intruders have made their way past the house. I don't know where they are. We hear the shots. Then the running. They are squatters from down near the river. All over the property they drop things: suitcases, computer monitors. The neighbour's house has been raided by the thieves, as a first port of call. The policeman stands panting and terrified on our doorstep.

–*I fired some warning shots*, he says. *I can't manage them all. I'm going now, ma'am. Dis genoeg vir my vanaand. Salanikahle. Good night all.*

–*No way. Not until you've checked out the neighbour's house and seen if people are dead or alive, and then checked out our place to see that no one's still hiding in the bushes.*

–*Okay*, he says, looking at my milk-soaked pyjamas and tear-stained cheeks. He's reluctant. Terrified. But my terror matches his notch for notch.

No one is dead. No one is injured. Perhaps he helps spare us all, the young policeman. Just in time. Or perhaps if he could have been down the road he might have spared the night of terror there, where men with AK-47s break through the burglar bars, terrorise a young mother, her eleven-month-old son and her husband the whole night, tying them up, and saying to each other:

–*Get the knife. Kill the baby. If he makes a noise, slice his throat.*

✡

I cannot imagine going to sleep every night and wondering whether you will be dead by sunrise.

Granny Bee and my dad arrive at the house in the morning to see the new baby. My son stares at the black and white stripes on his grandfather's shirt. Granny Bee's cheeks are pink and she wears the innocent smile of a girl who has been given some new and precious gift. She says:

*–My great-grandson. What incredible hands. I never thought I'd live long enough to see this day. Can I hold him?*

And when I place him in her arms, her eyes are wet.

*–Oh my, he's very heavy. Can you take him now?*

My dad kisses his head.

This is the last time I will see Granny Bee.

# Coda

The whispering score written into the DNA of Jacob David Frank is composed of a restless surge of blood which craves geographical sanctuary and healing.

In 2001 we are living back in America. Paul has found a job teaching at a community college, and I have healed from not being able to breathe. We have work visas and life has begun to resemble, as closely as possible, what we perceive to be normality. One afternoon, my dad calls me.

–*Granny Bee is dying*, he says. *She caught pneumonia. She's going in and out of consciousness.*

I sit down on the floor of our house and hold the phone to my ear. Not Granny Bee.

–*When God decides it's time, then that's how it is*, my dad says.

Pneumonia. I struggle to breathe.

–*She died peacefully*, my dad tells me a few days later. *Because of her heart condition she wasn't expected to live very long, you know. But she made it to eighty-four.*

The funeral of Bertha Frank Davidow in 2001 is a simple Jewish ceremony in Johannesburg attended by her sons and a few close friends. The rabbi describes her as a good person.

✡

Two years later, on the edge of the Gulf of Mexico, Tim begins to play the piano. His six-year-old hands have the controlled strength of an older person. He practises scales, devoted to each note; his focus is intense. He learns to sight-read without effort. Mr Miller would have approved. One day, he hears an organ being played in a church.

–*I want to do that*, he says.

The Holy Trinity Anglican Church is next to his school. In the morning, before school, I meet the organist.

–*Would you be interested in a young student?* I say. *He's only six, but since hearing the organ he thinks of nothing else.*

–*I'd be delighted. Bring him around this afternoon*, says Mr Cobb.

The great-great-grandson of Jacob David Frank begins to play the organ in America, under the tutelage of a benevolent, wise organist who can see the music that lives in a child's heart. The tunes and hymns have German names, and because Tim has an affinity for language, and learns German at school, he understands them and loves to say their names: *Abendstille*; *Es Tönen die Lieder, der Frühling kehrt Wieder.*

He learns to use both his hands and his feet. He tells me:

–*Everything there is to know about music, Bach knows. Mr Cobb is my teacher, but so is Bach.*

His organ teacher says one afternoon:

–*Have you heard your son? He can play a fugue. Do you know how uncanny this is? A fugue!*

Every day he can't wait to get to the church and up onto the organ bench. His feet barely reach the pedals and he has to hold on to his seat with his hands to do any footwork, in case he slides off. The church reverberates when he plays the deep C. His small body is engulfed by the sound his hands are making, and he becomes the music, disappearing into the resonance.

When he is nine he learns the famous *Toccata and Fugue in D minor.* While he is practising one day, the details of Bee's life bubble up under my skin and break through in tears, a storm at the end of the drought.

The music is around me. At the beginning of the toccata, I see the picture of a human life emerging. The different sections lead me through time, through childhood, adolescence and, with the beginning of the fugue, the journey into adulthood – here, the themes of childhood are echoed and transformed. And the phrase where all the threads come together, before old age approaches, is sad but also filled with passion for what has gone before.

The last minor chord hangs in the air, and I am in it, and my son is unaware of the universe of sound that holds the world in its embrace.

✡

I miss the stars of the Southern Hemisphere. I feel like a transplant in America. My body isn't well. My soul is restless.

When I was growing up in Africa, a Zulu medicine man told me that sometimes people will fall ill because they are not living beneath the right stars.

I look at the world map to see where the Southern Cross appears in the sky at night, and where the moon comes up with the same face it had in Africa. Then I apply for residence in Australia.

✡

My half-sister, ten years my junior, tells me that she spoke to a sangoma, a witchdoctor, in South Africa once. The sangoma told her that sometimes an ancestor will attach itself to a descendant in order to work through something that it could not complete itself in its lifetime. It will live vicariously through its descendant until some long-held grief or pattern is resolved.

I think of the orphanage and the university building in Wisconsin, and the sudden inability to breathe. I think of the feeling of having died in the Midwest and I take a step in an unexpected direction, dissolving the past.

I am granted permanent residence in Australia. After the struggle to be in America, the journey back to the Southern Hemisphere is simply an act of fate, a door opening in one direction rather than in another.

We leave everything in America. Our home, our cars, our jobs. We are not citizens and we have not allowed ourselves to take root – except for Tim's musical connection with the organist who teaches him.

We hold each other's hands, Paul and I, and in the shadows between our intertwined fingers lives the delicate whisper of a future waiting for its inception.

✡

From Australia, the moon does indeed look almost the same as in South Africa. The land is full of gum trees and succulents and afternoon thunderstorms. This is a land of power with its own tragedies and voices, which have been telling stories for a hundred thousand years. The ancient wisdom and culture of this country's scattered and dispossessed Indigenous people is a force that pulls me in and binds me to the land. I understand this country, although I have never been here before. I fall in love with the shape of the mountains, the smell of the air. The Southern Hemisphere sun reflects and breaks into a billion copies of itself in the shallow water on the Pacific shoreline, and reminds me of home. I look up at the stars at night and feel the Southern Cross pressing down on me. After a long search, I meet a revered Indigenous elder from the heart of the country, stolen eighty years ago from his parents by white men. I am haunted by his heartbreak, his dispossession of land, culture, family – his mother-loss. I ask for his permission to live here as an immigrant, to value and care for this, his country, his continent. And he tells me I can.

The tears that fall onto my new land are perhaps tears of relief, but my heart feels the shape of generations of dispossession and loss, and I am broken by the generosity of someone who has lost so much in a single lifetime.

Overhead, the Southern Hemisphere stars are the right way up. This unexpected land has soil into which my soul sinks hungry roots.

There are no lions here, no cheetahs or elephants. Strange marsupials bound across large green spaces and stop to stare at the humans passing by. Our nights are not punctuated with fear, and if I forget to lock the door when I leave the house, nothing happens.

It takes us two long years to find permanent jobs. For two years we consider that we have made a terrible mistake, followed a fatal pattern that will lead us nowhere. But then I get a teaching position in a high school, and Paul finally finds a job lecturing at a university. And the young organist with his remarkable fingers becomes a student of a renowned musician in Brisbane. The great-great-grandson of the Yiddish-speaking Jacob Frank falls in love with German hymns. He understands the words, but not why they move him. *Schmücke Dich, O Liebe Seele* and *Herzliebster Jesu* fill his heart.

*Herzliebster Jesu, was hast du verbrochen,*
*Daß man ein solch scharf Urteil hat gesprochen?*
*Was ist die Schuld? In was für Missetaten*
*Bist du geraten?*

Beloved Jesus, what have you done wrong
that they have pronounced so hard a sentence?
What is the blame for? What sort of misdeeds
are you being accused of?

And he loves everything by Johann Sebastian Bach. I listen to my son after his organ lesson. He is eleven. He says:

–*When you listen to Bach, every piece tells a story. It's a narrative. Vivaldi, though, just paints pictures … just moods and feelings without it going somewhere specific. Ma, you should play music.*

I have in my possession an old violin that has been carried across continents. It has been silent for decades and I doubt whether it has a voice any longer.

Driven by long-dead dreams, I look for a teacher.

The old man who watches me take the violin out of the case for the first time in thirty years can see that I am someone who feels there is no longer anything to lose. His eyes mist over when I tentatively manage the *Air on the G-string*. When he tells me to play anything I can remember with my eyes closed, I play *Hava Nagila* to the Australian winter light, while lorikeets screech in the background.

–*There is no limit to what you can do*, he says. *The only limit is the one you imagine.*

If he had been my teacher when I was younger, perhaps the music in me would not have stopped so abruptly. But perhaps I would not have met Paul and felt his music sink into my soul with such power.

And maybe the composition I longed to write, to be part of, has finally come into the world in an unexpected way.

I practise in the afternoons. My son is on the piano, explaining to me how to handle this phrase, or that one. I watch him transcend the boundaries of his inheritance and soar.

He takes up the double bass. At school, where he has been accepted into a music excellence program, he plays in every ensemble. Musical dreams that seem to have waited for generations burst into the world. He becomes the music captain at school. One day he says:

*–We're playing something really cool in strings. Here, I'll find it for you on YouTube.*

We hunch over the laptop. He hooks it up to the speakers so that we can get the full effect, and he presses play.

*–It's Handel's* Largo, he says. *Close your eyes and listen.*

I close my eyes. The chords well up in the living room, but also in my heart. The solemn aria, composed in 1738, was a failure when it was first played. A failure! Impossible to imagine how human beings were not moved by this for a hundred years. I want to weep for Handel. He left his soul in every phrase, in every part, every harmony. It took a century for the piece to find its audience. And suddenly everyone loved it.

I rest my chin in my hands and listen. The violins and flutes reach to the skies, supported by violas, cellos and a wide, expansive bass line, which goes through me on its way to the centre of the earth. The piece carries me above the web of time in which we are trapped unless we have the capacity to see beyond the linear. I am left somewhere far outside my small existence as a limited human being whose mission seems to have been trying to find home.

*–Ma, are you crying?*

✡

Later in the day, I hear him playing the *Largo* on the organ. And I think of the river of time flowing from the moment Bertha Frank was listening to the organ at her confirmation in Cleveland, Ohio, to the present, where her great-grandson plays it under Australian skies.

✡

In 2012, my great-uncle Mike dies at the age of ninety-four, having outlived his sister by more than a decade.

✡

And in 2014, I return to South Africa at short notice with Tim to see my dad.

I haven't stood on this earth for more than fifteen years. On the streets, in restaurants, cafes and bars and in the workplace, South Africa is indeed the most integrated place I have ever seen. The air, the trees, the sky remind me of my younger self. The mountains in Cape Town are giants. And yet violence ripples through lives and ravages communities and individuals with pervasive ferocity.

At dawn, Tim and I climb Table Mountain. The land of my son's birth tells him that the pulse of the continent is in his veins.

–*I love this place*, he says.

The smell of fynbos is all around us. Wind sweeps tumbling cascades of cloud through the ravine that we climb until we can't see in front of us. Huge boulders guard our passage to the summit. And we stand in slowly dissipating cloud, watching the world appear beneath us: the city; Robben Island, where Nelson Mandela spent most of his prison sentence; the wide carpet of ocean that stretches to the sky; the small house in Oranjezicht where my dad is waiting to see us.

The disease is turning his body to stone. He has no diagnosis, but my heart is a silent pit of fear. I sit at my father's feet and look at his wasted muscles. The oxygen machine pumps relief into his lungs because his diaphragm can no longer do what it is meant to do. A tumult is gathering in my heart, a thunderstorm. Presently, it will break.

He kisses Tim on the head. He kisses me. He says:

*–I love you all to an infinite degree.*

And he turns away from me.

✡

Tim and I leave Africa. Parts of our souls are tangled forever in the crevices of lichen-covered boulders on Table Mountain.

✡

My dad dies on the Easter weekend, which is also Pesach. He dies on my half-sister's Hebrew birthday, three weeks after being diagnosed with motor neurone disease. In two months he would have turned seventy-five.

✡

Struggling under the weight of loss, I ask a volunteer from the Motor Neurone Disease Society what possible cause there could have been for my father's cruel sentence.

*–We don't know,* she says. *The only factor that seems to be consistent with all MND patients is that at some earlier point in their lives they suffered a deep emotional trauma. Did he have that?*

*–Yes*, I say.

✡

Back in Australia, an indigo storm gathers over the Pacific and breaks over the beach. The heavens open and pour down as if they will never cease. Lightning tears the sky apart and the whisper of a story comes to an end in Africa.

The score is inscribed into the past century. From 1913 to 2014, the same melody has played itself out across the continents.

The morning after my dad's death, the sun comes up for the first time on a world that has not been without him in it since before he was born.

Time shatters into segments and surrounds me with images and words, and then I hear a fugue, played by a young boy in the music room next door. His hands liberate the story: not a single voice, but many, connected by a motif, a whispering that repeats itself over time, through generations, re-emerging, a contrapuntal development of journeys across oceans, of grief and loss and love and hope.

To my dearest Phillip
Bertha
10/21/37

*For Jacob David Frank*
*Bertha Frank Davidow*
*And my dad,*
*Robert Jack Davidow*
*June 22, 1939 – April 19, 2014*

# Acknowledgements

My thanks and gratitude to Alexandra Payne at UQP for your generosity of vision in seeing this book, and to editor Ian See for your invaluable advice. To Gary Crew, thanks for your wisdom at an important time.

There could be no memoir without the trust and support of my immediate family: to my dad, Bob Davidow (1939–2014), for your love, phone conversations and the gift of the box of letters that held the story. Thank you for trusting me to do things right. To my uncle, Woody Davidow, for the scans of Bee's diaries, which I did not know existed when I started writing. Paul Williams, my partner and most trusted and tireless critical reader, thank you for your honesty and belief in the value of this story. To my sister Amy Davidow, thank you for your feedback on the final manuscript; to my stepmother, Maureen Davidow, and my aunt, Marianne Davidow, for scans of old pictures. To my mother, Carol Liknaitzky, and my stepfather, David Liknaitzky, for bringing the box of letters safely from my dad's doorstep in South Africa to mine in Australia. To all my family, and to my brothers, Matthew Liknaitzky, Paul Liknaitzky, Larry Davidow, Jake Davidow, and my son, Tim Williams, for understanding the love that ties us all together across oceans and continents and over generations.

*In acknowledgement of the displaced –*
*And those who come after.*

# List of Images